Tony Blair

MODERN WORLD LEADERS

MODERN WORLD LEADERS

Tony Blair

Bonnie Hinman

CHELSEA HOUSE
PUBLISHERS

An imprint of Infobase Publishing

Tony Blair

Copyright © 2007 by Infobase Publishing

Chelsea House
An imprint of Infobase Publishing
132 West 31st Street
New York, NY 10001

Library of Congress Cataloging-in-Publication Data

Hinman, Bonnie.
  Tony Blair / Bonnie Hinman. — [Rev. ed.].
    p. cm. — (Modern world leaders)
  Includes bibliographical references and index.
  ISBN 0-7910-9216-X (hardcover)
  1. Blair, Tony, 1953—Juvenile literature. 2. Prime ministers—Great Britain—Biography—Juvenile literature. I. Title. II. Series.
  DA591.B56H46 2006
  941.085'9092—dc22   2006011017

Chelsea House books are available at special discounts when purchased in bulk quantities for businesses, associations, institutions, or sales promotions. Please call our Special Sales Department in New York at (212) 967-8800 or (800) 322-8755.

You can find Chelsea House on the World Wide Web at http://www.chelseahouse.com

Text design by Erik Lindstrom
Cover design by Takeshi Takahashi

Printed in the United States of America

Bang FOF 10 9 8 7 6 5 4 3 2 1

This book is printed on acid-free paper.

TABLE OF CONTENTS

ARTHUR M. SCHLESINGER, JR.

On Leadership

Leadership, it may be said, is really what makes the world go round. Love no doubt smoothes the passage; but love is a private transaction between consenting adults. Leadership is a public transaction with history. The idea of leadership affirms the capacity of individuals to move, inspire, and mobilize masses of people so that they act together in pursuit of an end. Sometimes leadership serves good purposes, sometimes bad; but whether the end is benign or evil, great leaders are those men and women who leave their personal stamp on history.

Now, the very concept of leadership implies the proposition that individuals can make a difference. This proposition has never been universally accepted. From classical times to the present day, eminent thinkers have regarded individuals as no more than the agents and pawns of larger forces, whether the gods and goddesses of the ancient world or, in the modern era, race, class, nation, the dialectic, the will of the people, the spirit of the times, history itself. Against such forces, the individual dwindles into insignificance.

So contends the thesis of historical determinism. Tolstoy's great novel *War and Peace* offers a famous statement of the case. Why, Tolstoy asked, did millions of men in the Napoleonic Wars, denying their human feelings and their common sense, move back and forth across Europe slaughtering their fellows? "The war," Tolstoy answered, "was bound to happen simply because it was bound to happen." All prior history determined it. As for leaders, they, Tolstoy said, "are but the labels that serve to give a name to an end and, like labels, they have the least possible connection with the event." The greater the leader, "the more conspicuous the inevitability and the predestination of every act he commits." The leader, said Tolstoy, is "the slave of history."

Determinism takes many forms. Marxism is the determinism of class. Nazism the determinism of race. But the idea of men and women as the slaves of history runs athwart the deepest human instincts. Rigid determinism abolishes the idea of human freedom—the assumption of free choice that underlies every move we make, every word we speak, every thought we think. It abolishes the idea of human responsibility, since it is manifestly unfair to reward or punish people for actions that are by definition beyond their control. No one can live consistently by any deterministic creed. The Marxist states prove this themselves by their extreme susceptibility to the cult of leadership.

More than that, history refutes the idea that individuals make no difference. In December 1931, a British politician crossing Fifth Avenue in New York City between 76th and 77th streets around 10:30 P.M. looked in the wrong direction and was knocked down by an automobile—a moment, he later recalled, of a man aghast, a world aglare: "I do not understand why I was not broken like an eggshell or squashed like a gooseberry." Fourteen months later an American politician, sitting in an open car in Miami, Florida, was fired on by an assassin; the man beside him was hit. Those who believe that individuals make no difference to history might well ponder whether the next two decades would have been the same had Mario Constasino's car killed Winston Churchill in 1931 and Giuseppe Zangara's bullet killed Franklin Roosevelt in 1933. Suppose, in addition, that Lenin had died of typhus in Siberia in 1895 and that Hitler had been killed on the western front in 1916. What would the twentieth century have looked like now?

For better or for worse, individuals do make a difference. "The notion that a people can run itself and its affairs anonymously," wrote the philosopher William James, "is now well known to be the silliest of absurdities. Mankind does nothing save through initiatives on the part of inventors, great or small, and imitation by the rest of us—these are the sole factors in human progress. Individuals of genius show the way, and set the patterns, which common people then adopt and follow."

Leadership, James suggests, means leadership in thought as well as in action. In the long run, leaders in thought may well make the greater difference to the world. "The ideas of economists and political philosophers, both when they are right and when they are wrong," wrote John Maynard Keynes, "are more powerful than is commonly understood. Indeed the world is ruled by little else. Practical men, who believe themselves to be quite exempt from any intellectual influences, are usually the slaves of some defunct economist. . . . The power of vested interests is vastly exaggerated compared with the gradual encroachment of ideas."

But, as Woodrow Wilson once said, "Those only are leaders of men, in the general eye, who lead in action. . . . It is at their hands that new thought gets its translation into the crude language of deeds." Leaders in thought often invent in solitude and obscurity, leaving to later generations the tasks of imitation. Leaders in action—the leaders portrayed in this series—have to be effective in their own time.

And they cannot be effective by themselves. They must act in response to the rhythms of their age. Their genius must be adapted, in a phrase from William James, "to the receptivities of the moment." Leaders are useless without followers. "There goes the mob," said the French politician, hearing a clamor in the streets. "I am their leader. I must follow them." Great leaders turn the inchoate emotions of the mob to purposes of their own. They seize on the opportunities of their time, the hopes, fears, frustrations, crises, potentialities. They succeed when events have prepared the way for them, when the community is awaiting to be aroused, when they can provide the clarifying and organizing ideas. Leadership completes the circuit between the individual and the mass and thereby alters history.

It may alter history for better or for worse. Leaders have been responsible for the most extravagant follies and most monstrous crimes that have beset suffering humanity. They have also been vital in such gains as humanity has made in individual freedom, religious and racial tolerance, social justice, and respect for human rights.

There is no sure way to tell in advance who is going to lead for good and who for evil. But a glance at the gallery of men and women in MODERN WORLD LEADERS suggests some useful tests.

One test is this: Do leaders lead by force or by persuasion? By command or by consent? Through most of history leadership was exercised by the divine right of authority. The duty of followers was to defer and to obey. "Theirs not to reason why/Theirs but to do and die." On occasion, as with the so-called enlightened despots of the eighteenth century in Europe, absolutist leadership was animated by humane purposes. More often, absolutism nourished the passion for domination, land, gold, and conquest and resulted in tyranny.

The great revolution of modern times has been the revolution of equality. "Perhaps no form of government," wrote the British historian James Bryce in his study of the United States, *The American Commonwealth*, "needs great leaders so much as democracy." The idea that all people should be equal in their legal condition has undermined the old structure of authority, hierarchy, and deference. The revolution of equality has had two contrary effects on the nature of leadership. For equality, as Alexis de Tocqueville pointed out in his great study *Democracy in America*, might mean equality in servitude as well as equality in freedom.

"I know of only two methods of establishing equality in the political world," Tocqueville wrote. "Rights must be given to every citizen, or none at all to anyone . . . save one, who is the master of all." There was no middle ground "between the sovereignty of all and the absolute power of one man." In his astonishing prediction of twentieth-century totalitarian dictatorship, Tocqueville explained how the revolution of equality could lead to the *Führerprinzip* and more terrible absolutism than the world had ever known.

But when rights are given to every citizen and the sovereignty of all is established, the problem of leadership takes a new form, becomes more exacting than ever before. It is easy to issue commands and enforce them by the rope and the stake, the concentration camp and the *gulag*. It is much harder to use argument and achievement to overcome opposition and win consent. The Founding Fathers of the United States understood the difficulty. They believed that history had given them the opportunity to decide, as Alexander Hamilton wrote in the first Federalist Paper, whether men are indeed capable of basing government on "reflection and choice, or whether they are forever destined to depend . . . on accident and force."

Government by reflection and choice called for a new style of leadership and a new quality of followership. It required leaders to be responsive to popular concerns, and it required followers to be active and informed participants in the process. Democracy does not eliminate emotion from politics; sometimes it fosters demagoguery; but it is confident that, as the greatest of democratic leaders put it, you cannot fool all of the people all of the time. It measures leadership by results and retires those who overreach or falter or fail.

It is true that in the long run despots are measured by results too. But they can postpone the day of judgment, sometimes indefinitely, and in the meantime they can do infinite harm. It is also true that democracy is no guarantee of virtue and intelligence in government, for the voice of the people is not necessarily the voice of God. But democracy, by assuring the right of opposition, offers built-in resistance to the evils inherent in absolutism. As the theologian Reinhold Niebuhr summed it up, "Man's capacity for justice makes democracy possible, but man's inclination to justice makes democracy necessary."

A second test for leadership is the end for which power is sought. When leaders have as their goal the supremacy of a master race or the promotion of totalitarian revolution or the acquisition and exploitation of colonies or the protection of greed and privilege or the preservation of personal power, it is likely that their leadership will do little to advance the cause of humanity. When their goal is the abolition of slavery, the liberation of women, the enlargement of opportunity for the poor and powerless, the extension of equal rights to racial minorities, the defense of the freedoms of expression and opposition, it is likely that their leadership will increase the sum of human liberty and welfare.

Leaders have done great harm to the world. They have also conferred great benefits. You will find both sorts in this series. Even "good" leaders must be regarded with a certain wariness. Leaders are not demigods; they put on their trousers one leg after another just like ordinary mortals. No leader is infallible, and every leader needs to be reminded of this at regular intervals. Irreverence irritates leaders but is their salvation. Unquestioning submission corrupts leaders and demeans followers. Making a cult of a leader is always a mistake. Fortunately hero worship generates its own antidote. "Every hero," said Emerson, "becomes a bore at last."

The single benefit the great leaders confer is to embolden the rest of us to live according to our own best selves, to be active, insistent, and resolute in affirming our own sense of things. For great leaders attest to the reality of human freedom against the supposed inevitabilities of history. And they attest to the wisdom and power that may lie within the most unlikely of us, which is why Abraham Lincoln remains the supreme example of great leadership. A great leader, said Emerson, exhibits new possibilities to all humanity. "We feed on genius. . . . Great men exist that there may be greater men."

Great leaders, in short, justify themselves by emancipating and empowering their followers. So humanity struggles to master its destiny, remembering with Alexis de Tocqueville: "It is true that around every man a fatal circle is traced beyond which he cannot pass; but within the wide verge of that circle he is powerful and free; as it is with man, so with communities." ●

1

London
Under Attack

THE FIRST WEEK OF JULY 2005 HAD BEEN A GOOD ONE FOR BRITAIN AND its prime minister, Tony Blair. London had been awarded the Summer Olympic Games for 2012, winning over cities like Paris and New York. The annual G8 summit meeting among the eight leading industrialized nations was starting in Gleneagles, Scotland. As this year's host and chairman, Tony Blair had planned an agenda of prickly issues to be discussed. Blair hoped to find some common ground with other nations about global climate change and African poverty.

Thursday morning, July 7, found Blair meeting with President George Bush as the summit began. He was meeting with the Chinese prime minister when disturbing reports from London began to arrive. There had been some kind of explosion in the subway, or tube as it is called in London. Early information indicated that there may have been one or more power surges in the grid that supplied the underground trains.

Aides informed Blair of the events after his meeting. Confusion over the cause of the explosion continued for several hours before it became clear that there had been four explosions and that they were likely terrorist acts. During this time, Blair continued with his scheduled meetings and was updated regularly.

Shortly after noon, a grim-faced Blair gave an initial statement from Gleneagles. In part, he said, "It's reasonably clear there have been a series of terrorist attacks in London. There are, obviously, casualties, both people that have died and people seriously injured. And our thoughts and prayers, of course, are with the victims and their families."

Referring to the G8 agenda, Blair went on to say, "It's particularly barbaric that this has happened on a day when people are meeting to try to help the problems of poverty in Africa and the long-term problems of climate change in the environment."

"There will be time to talk later about this," he continued. "It's important, however, that those engaged in terrorism realize that our determination to defend our values and our way of life is greater than their determination to cause death and destruction to innocent people in a desire to impose extremism on the world."

Plans were under way for Blair to go down to London as bad news from that city continued to come in a steady stream. There had been three explosions in the tube, and one destroyed a double-decker bus. The three tube explosions had occurred within less than a minute of each other, and the bus was blown up about an hour later. Rescue efforts by the police and firefighters proceeded at top speed as many victims were trapped far underground in the tube tunnels.

Meanwhile, Blair informed Bush and the other leaders and asked them to proceed with the summit while he returned to London to meet with his emergency team. They agreed and issued a joint statement about the bombings.

Less than one hour before bombing the number 30 double-decker bus (above) in Tavistock Square, London, suicide bomber Hasib Hussain strolled nonchalantly around the city. The July 7, 2005, attack struck fear in the hearts of people in London and around the world.

Blair once more appeared before the cameras, but this time, he was flanked by President George Bush and French leader Jacques Chirac with the other leaders standing behind them. Blair read a statement from the summit participants. "We will not allow violence to change our societies or our values. Nor will we let it stop the work of this summit. We will continue our deliberations in the interests of a better world. The terrorists will not succeed . . . We shall prevail and they shall not."

Foreign Secretary Jack Straw chaired the G8 talks while Blair returned to London. More information about the attacks was arriving minute by minute at the emergency services center. The center and the officials who man it are called COBRA (Cabinet Office Briefing Room A). This high-level crisis management team is activated only in the case of a national emergency.

Prime Minister Blair arrived back in London in the afternoon and went directly to a meeting of COBRA. By the time the meeting convened, BBC News had reported that it had discovered a claim of responsibility on a Web site known to be operated by al Qaeda associates. This group called itself the "Secret Organisation—al-Qaeda in Europe" and claimed the attacks were a response to Britain's participation in the 2003 invasion of Iraq.

Blair obtained an update on rescue operations, police investigations, and the state of the transit system as thousands of Londoners started their evening commute. Rumors of other bombs continued to disrupt the transit services, making it necessary for many commuters to walk home or stay in their offices.

Blair emerged from his meeting to offer another statement about the bombings and their aftermath. "There has been a most terrible and tragic atrocity that has cost many innocent lives. I would like again to express my profound condolences to the families of the victims, and to those who are casualties of this terrorist act."

Upon hearing the news of the bomb attacks in London, Tony Blair exits the G8 Summit in Gleneagles, Scotland, on July 7, 2005. Blair rejoined the meeting that evening.

Blair knew that much of his audience would have heard about al Qaeda's claim of responsibility, so he was careful to point out that the vast majority of Muslims in Britain and elsewhere are law-abiding and hate terrorism just as much as any Briton or American.

The prime minister finished his statement with the kind of ringing words for which he has long been famous. "When they try to intimidate us, we will not be intimidated. When they seek to change our country or our way of life by these methods, we will not be changed. When they try to divide our people or weaken our resolve, we will not be divided and our resolve will hold firm."

Within hours, the day of the bombings was being called simply 7/7, just as the terrorist attacks in the United States on September 11, 2001, came to be called 9/11. Blair must have long expected that his country would have to face such attacks. London is a global financial center, and Britain is a strong ally of the United States. Blair himself has often been the glue that holds the U.S.–British alliance together.

In what sometimes seems an unlikely partnership given the differences in their political parties, Tony Blair and George Bush have stood shoulder to shoulder in the war on terror. This partnership may illustrate Tony Blair's worldview better than any policy statement ever could. He's not overly concerned about political parties or ideologies when it comes to international terrorism or any other event or problem that faces mankind. We stand together or we fall into chaos together might be his motto.

2

Birth of a Leader

ANTHONY CHARLES LYNTON BLAIR WAS BORN IN EDINBURGH, SCOTLAND, on May 6, 1953. His parents, Leo and Hazel Blair, soon moved the new baby and their older child, William, to Glasgow. Mr. Blair was a junior tax inspector and studied at night for a law degree. Late in 1954, Leo Blair was offered a position at the University of Adelaide in Australia. It was an important move professionally, so the family packed its belongings and sailed to Australia on the ocean liner *Iberia*. According to family lore as told by Leo Blair, toddler Tony was a show-off. The Blairs traveled first-class, and Tony entertained their fellow passengers by dancing as the band played. The dance ended, the elder Blair said, only when Tony's diaper dropped to his ankles.

In Adelaide, Tony's sister, Sarah, was born, and Tony continued to enjoy the performer's life. His father tells of a concert at Tony's school at which the four-year-old danced and sang and generally brought down the house.

After three years, the Blairs moved to Durham, in northern England, where Leo had a job at Durham University. Leo also studied to take the English Bar Exam and became active in local Conservative Party politics.

Tony went to Western Hill pre-prep school and at the age of eight joined his brother at Chorister School in Durham, a public school, where they were daytime students, or "day boys." What is known as a public school in Great Britain is actually the same as a private school elsewhere. The Blairs weren't wealthy, but the hard-working lawyer could afford to send his sons to the reasonably priced Chorister School.

Tony did well in school and excelled athletically. He played cricket and rugby, even winning the school's Scott Cup as best rugby player for 1965–1966. He continued his career in entertainment as a spear-carrier in a school play. He loved to read and enjoyed C.S. Lewis's Chronicles of Narnia series and J.R.R. Tolkien's *The Lord of the Rings*. Tony and his father often attended football games (Americans call this sport soccer).

Early summer vacations were spent in Ireland. His mother came from Ballyshannon on the Irish coast. The Blairs stayed at a hotel in nearby Rossnowlagh. Tony learned to swim there, and it was there that his father took him to his first pub. The head of Chorister School, Canon Grove, remembers Tony as a smiling, good sort of boy to have in a prep school, polite and well-mannered. Blair has related that his parents believed strongly in the importance of good manners. "They always said, 'Misbehave inside the family if you will, but outside make us proud of you.' If I was told off at school, I was told off again at home."

Tony and the other Blairs had a comfortable middle-class life, but the direction of their lives changed when Tony was 11 years old. Leo Blair, who was 40 and about to run for a Conservative parliamentary seat, suffered a stroke.

On July 4, 1964, Tony's mother awakened him. He knew that something dreadful had happened even before his mother

When Tony was 12, he made a start on his political career by volunteering to stand as the Conservative candidate in a mock election at his school.

told him that his father had been taken to the hospital. Friends arrived to take Tony to school, where he spent the day not knowing whether his father would survive.

His mother came to pick him up after a rugby game that afternoon and gave her son the good news that his father would probably live. Later, Tony referred to July 4, 1964, as "the day my childhood ended." Leo Blair did survive, but he returned from the hospital unable to talk or walk.

Tony's mother was a hero to her son. She took care of her husband and gradually taught him to talk again. In a few months, Leo Blair was able to walk and get around, but speaking took much longer. The frustration was huge for a man who had planned to begin a career in politics. Blair has said that it was at this time that his father transferred his own political ambitions to his children.

A further burden on Hazel Blair and the family came when eight-year-old Sarah developed Still's disease, a juvenile form of rheumatoid arthritis. Just as Leo began to improve, Sarah's illness worsened. She was in the hospital for two years, receiving various drugs. Mrs. Blair coped as best she could with overwhelming responsibility.

The Blairs had to tighten their belts financially, but the boys continued at their schools, and owing to their mother's efforts, life went on largely as usual. When Tony was 12, he made a start on his political career by volunteering to stand as the Conservative candidate in a mock election at his school. Perhaps fate intervened to prevent him from standing as a Conservative, even for a mock election—Tony was ill that day, and another student took over.

BLAIR AND SCHOOLING

As was common in British middle- and upper-class families, Tony was sent to boarding school when he was 13. His parents had already sent William to Fettes College in Edinburgh, Scotland. Tony won a small scholarship and began his boarding school days in Kimmerghame House, where his brother had begun. It was here that for the first time Tony became something of a problem student.

Tony hated being away from home and disliked the harsh discipline and custom known as "fagging," in which junior boys were used as servants to seniors. Tony was required to clean his prefect's shoes, polish brass, and make toast, among other duties. The older boys were allowed to cane the junior boys, even for relatively minor offenses. Tony performed his duties cheerfully enough but hated the whole business.

One positive note for Tony was his English teacher, Eric Anderson. Anderson shaped much of Tony's experience at Fettes. Toward the end of the year, Anderson announced that he would be heading up a new house the next year. Volunteers were asked to join together at the new house, which was to be called Arniston. Tony was desperate to be chosen for the new house, and Anderson made sure that he was.

Still, even that prospect seems not to have reconciled Tony to his life at school; he ran away as he was returning for his second year. Apparently, when his parents put him on the train at Newcastle-upon-Tyne, he simply walked through the train cars and climbed off at the other end of the platform. The 14-year-old boy got to the Newcastle airport and managed to get on a plane before he was stopped. The school was called, and they alerted Tony's parents.

It was just the first battle in Tony's war with school authorities and his father. The elder Blair had recovered from his stroke just in time to deal with a rebellious teenage son. The failed escape plan was the most visible sign of Tony's rebellion, but he delighted in challenging any and all school rules. Some of the rules were rather petty even in Tony's new house, which abolished caning and changed the fagging procedures. One hated and much ignored rule was that a student must keep the middle button of his jacket buttoned at all times. The masters or teachers spent a lot of time enforcing the jacket-button rule, as well as scores of rules about where the boys could be at any given time.

As might be expected, the boys spent an equal amount of time trying to find ways around the rules. It was particularly attractive to sneak away from school grounds to go to the shops or pubs for snacks. Even more important, Tony and the other boys searched for opportunities to chat with the local girls.

Tony played sports, including basketball, which was natural for him because he was tall. The school activity he seemed to enjoy the most was acting. At 14, he was chosen to play Marc Antony in *Julius Caesar*. Other roles in school plays followed, with generally good reviews by the school paper. The highlight of his dramatic career was probably his final role. He played a company commander in a drama set in the trenches of World War I. The commander found himself unable to endure the horrors of war without ample whiskey. It was a good role for a young rebel who participated in the school cadet force only when that participation was required.

According to David Kennedy, Arniston house tutor, Tony questioned everything at Fettes. It appeared that Tony was an intellectual rebel rather than just a troublemaker. "Some boys are rebellious because they are stupid," Kennedy has said. "Tony was rebellious because he wanted to question all the values we held to."

The path wasn't easy, though, and life became particularly difficult when the understanding Eric Anderson left Arniston for a job elsewhere. His successor as housemaster, Bob Roberts, was stricter and on the whole found Tony, who was in his last year, to be absolutely infuriating. Tony certainly tried the housemaster's patience with his disregard for rules and just passable respectfulness. Before the year's end, Roberts had beaten Tony for persistent flouting of school rules. Tony had escaped such punishment before, and indeed it was unusual to whip a 17-year-old, even at a school as conservative as Fettes.

In the midst of a difficult final year, Tony still managed to pass his exams but barely avoided being expelled. His Fettes career ended on a bad note, much as it had begun. He had made a place for himself, but it probably wasn't the happiest time of his life. In spite of the difficulties, he had obtained a solid education, and he was now ready to tackle the world of university. But first he would take a year off. This year, commonly called "the gap year," has been one of the privileges of some youth in Britain. The year off is supposed to introduce a young person to the real world. Tony was anxious to experience that real world.

A MAJOR CHANGE IN PLANS

Tony Blair's "gap year" showed little that would indicate his future career path in politics. In the fall of 1971, he went off to London. There he knocked on the door of Alan Collenette, who was a friend of a friend. Tony had heard that Alan was a rock-band promoter. Tony suggested that the pair go into business together.

Tony claimed to be a guitarist, but it soon became apparent that while he did have a guitar, he hadn't quite learned to play it yet. Collenette said later that Tony's lack of skill wasn't too important, as Collenette himself wasn't much of a rock promoter.

What Tony did possess was great enthusiasm and persuasiveness. Alan was convinced, and the pair eventually sat down at the kitchen table of the Collenette family home and planned their career. Their intent was to discover, promote, and manage the next Led Zeppelin. But rock promoters need a band. Alan had just left St. Paul's school in London and had a guitar-playing friend, Mike Sheppard, who was still at school. Mike's father would let the prospective band rehearse in the Sheppard home's basement. Mike recruited Adam Sieff, who was a member of Jaded, a band that had recently broken up. The band was reformed with Sheppard, Sieff, and a few other friends.

Blair-Collenette Promotions now had a band but still needed a place to perform, preferably a cheap place. Norman Burt, a part-time deacon at the Vineyard Congregationalist Church in Richmond, agreed to let the would-be promoters use the church hall for performances. Burt ran a youth club there, so he was interested in reaching out to young people.

Transportation for the promoters was an old blue Ford Thames van that Tony had bought for £50. They hauled bands and equipment around London, on one occasion losing a wheel as they rounded a corner. The van also allowed Blair-Collenette Promotions to earn a bit of extra money, since rock promoting, while satisfying, was not particularly lucrative. Tony kept the books, which showed a modest profit from their operations. They took on other work, including deliveries and stocking shelves at a grocery store.

Tony did sing the occasional song at the Vineyard, but most of the time he took money, handled lights, and did some disc jockeying. He dressed the part in tight flared jeans and striped jacket, topped with a brown fur coat. The overall look was scruffy in a carefully constructed way.

THE END OF THAT DREAM

By May 1972, Tony and Alan wanted to move up in the rock promotion world. Although they had been reasonably successful, they had to admit that there probably wasn't a future in rock promoting for Tony and his partner. There may have been regrets, but the partners knew that it was time for Tony to head for Oxford and for Alan to find a real job.

Tony may have shown no interest in politics, but the personality and character that fueled his gap year as a rock promoter would stand him in good stead later. He was resourceful, hard working, and had a sense of humor. What he didn't do during that time is important as well. He didn't take illegal drugs or smoke marijuana, even though both were readily available in the London music crowd in 1971. He apparently didn't drink to excess nor have any brushes with the local police.

In one respect Tony went strongly upstream from the crowd. Collenette recalled that his friend and business partner was a Christian believer. "He was God-fearing and that was unusual at that time in that circle of people. I respected him greatly for it." These Christian beliefs were to play a strong role later as Tony developed the social conscience that propelled him into politics.

St. John's College, a part of Oxford University, welcomed the former rock promoter in the fall of 1972. Tony followed family tradition like his father and brother and studied law. He was rather more flamboyant in actions and appearance than his fellow students of law, although he stayed well within school boundaries. Tony's father told of going to pick up his son at Oxford that first year only to be greeted by an interestingly dressed stranger who turned out to be his son. It was probably the shoulder-length hair, open shirt, and black synthetic-skin coat with red lining that fooled the elder Blair.

One of the more talked about parts of Tony's Oxford days was his stint as lead singer for a rock band called Ugly Rumours. The existing band felt they needed to perk up their charisma level and offered an audition to Tony. In typical fashion, and unlike the usual prospective rock band singer, Tony learned the words to several of the band's songs before auditioning. He was offered the spot immediately.

The bass guitarist, Mark Ellen, has since described Tony's immediate impact on Ugly Rumours. "I was amazed by how keen he was on the idea of rehearsal. I think we were just a little bit looser—'Hey, we'll just turn up and we'll be brilliant.'"

By all accounts, the band's first performance was the most memorable. Tony was deep into his Mick Jagger imitations during the third song when the drums began to fall off the drum riser. One by one, they rolled off the stage and onto the floor. The Ugly Rumours were horrified and just looked at each other at first. Then Tony grabbed the microphone and chatted with the audience, killing time until the others could get the drums reassembled. Ellen remembers standing in the back, watching Tony work the audience and thinking, "This is no ordinary junior love-god lead singer we have here. Where is this guy going to go?"

At Oxford, there were certain things an aspiring politician might do. He would certainly have a role in the Oxford Union, and he probably would join the University Labour Club. Chances are, he would write thought-provoking articles for the student newspapers.

Tony wasn't thinking about student politics and causes, but he was thinking. Like most of his contemporaries in the 1970s, Tony was antiestablishment and liberal in his ideas. He read widely and argued over philosophy at every opportunity.

Tony met a young man at Oxford who deeply influenced his politics and life, seemingly more than any other one person. Peter Thomson was an Australian minister for the Anglican Church. He had come to Oxford to fulfill a dream of studying theology at St. John's College. At 36, Thomson was older and had a little more money than did the younger students he met. He had gathered a group of young friends who congregated in his room to smoke his cigarettes and drink his coffee while discussing how to solve the world's problems. Tony became part of that group.

Thomson was considered by the others to be a Christian socialist who wanted to discuss endlessly how moral philosophy could be put into practice. He was open-minded and charismatic, and the student-members of the ongoing forum he established generally leaned toward Marxism or at least were extremely liberal. It seems to have been at these late-night sessions that Tony formed the political views that have guided him ever since.

Tony Blair's education at Oxford University prepared him for his future as a world leader.

Thomson introduced Tony to a Scottish philosopher, John Macmurray. The height of Macmurray's popularity had come in the 1930s, but he had much to say about the idea of community that was still relevant 40 years later. He believed that by working for the whole community we benefit all the individuals within it, including ourselves.

With this philosophy in mind, Peter Thomson tied his religious beliefs firmly to his political ideas. He believed that sincerely following Christian principles would lead directly to the betterment of the community as a whole and thus to individual gain.

It was an idea that held great appeal for Tony. He later said that while he had indeed always believed in God, he hadn't been able to make sense of his beliefs. He said that Peter made religion relevant and practical. Tony's approach to life had always been practical so this idea of serving God by serving community caused his political beliefs to fall into place. He said, "My Christianity and my politics came together at the same time."

By the end of his second year at Oxford, Tony was regularly attending services at the chapel and had asked to be confirmed in the Church of England. This was accomplished, and he has regularly attended church services ever since.

Tony wasn't immediately sure how he could use his desire to make a difference in the world within the existing political parties. Students of the early 1970s were strongly against mainstream politics, and it would have been very unfashionable to join any political party. The Labour Party was bogged down in arguments over involvement with Europe and which monopolies to nationalize. Marxism still dominated leftist political thought among students. Blair has said that he read the work of Trotsky and attempted to understand Marxism but found it unsatisfactory.

Tony's developing political ideas never did find any strong mode of expression while he was at St. John's College. He took part in a couple of demonstrations but nothing more concretely political than that. He has since said that the first issue that moved him politically was the antiapartheid movement. This is certainly in line with his sense of community and the personal responsibility that he thought should accompany any community's actions.

Professor John Macmurray's belief in the value of community helped connect Blair's interests in politics and religion and solidified his desire to make a difference in the world.

Tony graduated from St. John's College in June 1975. His beliefs were still developing, but he was definitely leaning toward the Labour Party as the way to change the world.

Hazel Blair, Tony's mother, died two weeks after graduation. She was 52 and had been diagnosed with throat cancer while Tony was still at Fettes. She had been successfully treated at first, and the Blairs had hidden the seriousness of her recurrence from their son so he wouldn't be distracted during exams. Leo Blair met Tony at the train station and broke the news to his son. The father and son went directly to the hospital.

Blair has said that his mother knew she was dying and talked to each of her children. She told each child what she expected of him or her. "I was always the wildest of the three [and] Mum was worried I might go off the rails. Also she was very anxious that we were a credit to Dad. She was insistent on us promising that we'd get ourselves sorted out and not do stupid things."

Tony was close to his mother and spoke later of the effect her early death had on him. "As well as your grief for the person, your own mortality comes home to you. And you suddenly realize—which often you don't as a young person—that life is finite, so if you want to get things done you had better get a move on." Tony did "get a move on." "My life took on an urgency," he has said, "which has probably never left it." The autumn of 1975 found him off to London once again. Law school was the next step toward living out his ideas.

3

Entering Politics

BLAIR'S ONE-YEAR LAW COURSE AT LINCOLN'S INN BEGAN IN SEPTEMBER 1975.
He began searching for an apprenticeship at the beginning of
1976. Law students who pass the bar exam had to serve an
apprenticeship, or pupilage, to gain work experience before
they could practice as lawyers. Apprentices were not paid then
but were sometimes offered scholarships.

Blair was waiting for a scholarship interview when he
noticed a dark-haired young woman standing next to him in
the alphabetically ordered line. Cherie Booth had graduated
from the London School of Economics with high honors and
was also interested in politics. There was no immediate friendship, but the two took notice of each other.

Blair and Booth soon had more in common than alpha-
betical order when the pupilages were announced. Blair had
applied a little late to work in the chambers of Derry Irvine, a
barrister who specialized in employment law. Irvine had already

taken on one pupil, Cherie Booth, but agreed to interview Blair on the recommendation of a mutual friend. Irvine said he was bowled over with Blair's enthusiasm and agreed to take on the second pupil.

Bar exams were necessary first steps. Booth scored at the top in the exams given in the summer of 1976, and she began her pupilage immediately. Blair, however, who passed his exams, too, went to France for the summer.

Blair worked in the bar of a hotel in Paris, where he got good tips from the American tourists because he spoke English. Many years later, he recalled that he received his first lesson in applied socialism when he began work at the bar. "The others told me to put all my tips into a communal pot. But at the end of the night I discovered it was only me who had been putting my money in."

BLAIR'S PUPILAGE

In the fall, Blair began his pupilage. He and Booth were locked in an intense competition to obtain a permanent position at Irvine's chambers. They both knew that only one apprentice would be awarded a tenancy at the end of their pupilage year. The competition could have driven them apart but instead made them closer. New Years 1977 found Blair and Booth regarding each other as more than fellow lawyers and adversaries. Eventually Booth broke up with her boyfriend and began to date Blair.

With the summer came the appointment of Blair to a tenancy with Irvine. Booth joined the chambers of George Carman, a famous libel lawyer. Blair had won both the tenancy and the girl. The next couple of years were a period of hard work with long hours for Blair. He sometimes went into his office as early as 6:30 A.M. to begin work. Rare leisure hours were spent with Booth, who was also working hard.

Blair had joined the Chelsea Labour Party when he moved to London and eventually transferred his membership to the

Fairfield branch of the Battersea Labour Party when he moved in with fellow lawyer Charles Falconer early in 1979.

In Great Britain's parliamentary system, elections are called at the direction of the party in power. They may be called at any time but must be held at least every five years. Headed by the prime minister, the government tries to time an election to occur when the members in control judge there to be the best chance of winning that election.

Sometimes there are miscalculations, and one of these led to the defeat of the Labour Party in the election called for May 3, 1979. Prime Minister James Callaghan was turned out of office and replaced by Margaret Thatcher, the Conservative Party leader. The Labour Party was destined to be out of power for 18 years after this defeat.

Blair's first public profession of political opinion was in an article written for the *Spectator* and published in August 1979. Blair offered a hard-hitting analysis of the arbitrary powers held by the immigration service. Several other articles followed over the next couple of years, most of which were written for the *New Statesman* about employment law.

Blair and Booth became engaged in the summer of 1979 and were married in the following March. The Blairs honeymooned in Italy and returned to live in Hackney. It was from Hackney that both Blair and Booth launched their political careers. At first it looked as if Booth might be the politician in the family. She had been a Labour Party member since she was 17 and had long aspired to be elected to Parliament.

Blair made his first try at getting elected to the House of Commons just a few months after moving to Hackney. He obtained a nomination from a branch of the electricians' union in Middlesbrough, which was near his boyhood home of Durham. However, the young politician failed to make the cut, so he returned to Hackney to work in a different direction.

Blair campaigned for and won election as secretary at the local-branch level. From there, he began to slowly build support, and made a couple more unsuccessful attempts to get nominated. Booth herself made one try in Crosby.

In April 1982, Blair won his first nomination to run in Beaconsfield in a by-election. It was considered a safe Conservative Party seat, but it was a start. The Labour Party's chances were dimmed by the surge of support for Prime Minister Margaret Thatcher when Argentina invaded the Falkland Islands on April 2. Labour was in a bad position because any criticism of the war would be seen as unpatriotic. In that atmosphere, Blair's showing wasn't particularly strong, but it had more to do with his party choice than his personal qualities. Party leaders all the way to the top noticed him and that would prove to be the real value of his candidacy.

Blair spent the next year tending to his lawyer duties and working in the midst of turbulent party politics. The Labour Party seemed on the verge of destroying itself, with different factions calling for opposite changes in party policy. In the midst of these disagreements, redistricting had scrambled some of the formerly safe Labour constituencies. In some instances, this left current members of Parliament looking for new districts. It was into this political whirlpool that Tony Blair jumped with both feet in May 1983.

EARLY POLITICAL AMBITIONS

On May 9, Prime Minister Thatcher called a general election for June 9. On May 11, Blair knocked on the door of a small house in Trimdon in County Durham. John Burton, party secretary for the Trimdon Village branch, welcomed Blair into what looked like a party to watch a football match on television. Blair had phoned Burton earlier to say that he had noticed that Trimdon hadn't nominated a candidate and asked if he could talk to the party leaders about becoming their nominee. Burton instructed Blair to come over to a meeting several members were having that night.

Former prime minister, Conservative Party leader Margaret Thatcher, waves from Number 10, Downing Street, the traditional residence of Britain's top elected official. The photograph was taken on May 5, 1979, two days after the Labour Party's defeat.

By John Burton's account, Tony Blair, who spoke last, "was brilliant, excellent— energetic and alive with ideas."

The meeting was held to do a postelection wrap-up after local elections the week before, but the important item of business was to watch the European Cup Winners' Cup final between Aberdeen and Real Madrid on television. Blair joined them, and waited for the opportunity to plead his case. After the Aberdeen team won in overtime, the five Trimdon party leaders turned to Blair and asked why they should nominate him.

By later accounts, Blair did a fairly good job of presenting his views. The group wasn't bowled over, but they liked the young man who had just turned 30. His ideas seemed reasonable and in line with their own, and John Burton thought that there might just be something special about the good-looking, personable Blair.

The group decided to give it a go, and eventually became known as the "Sedgefield posse." These five men threw themselves into getting Blair selected and provided a core of support that would carry their young candidate all the way to the top in the following years.

Getting Blair into the race began at the most basic level. The "posse" took turns driving Blair around to meet delegates to the selection conference. They provided lodging and lent him a car. Burton called a meeting of the Trimdon Village branch of the Sedgefield Labour Party for the following Saturday. Blair had to secure a nomination before he could even be considered for selection.

Blair spoke to the Trimdon meeting and received their nomination. The selection conference would be held less than a week later. Blair told the delegates that he realized that this

Left-wing MP Les Huckfield, shown here in August 1967, was Blair's principal opponent for Sedgefield Labour Party's nomination in 1983. Blair finally defeated him, 73 votes to 46. While MP, Huckfield worked for his brother's haulage business when Parliament was not in session.

late in the process they might have already decided to support a candidate, but would they consider supporting him if their first choice dropped off in the early rounds of voting.

Blair had one opponent who could spoil the whole deal. Les Huckfield was a left-wing member of Parliament (MP) who was looking for a new district and had strong support to take Sedgefield. In fact, he probably would have won easily if Sedgefield hadn't been a new constituency and still rather fluid politically.

Blair first managed to make the short list. On Friday night, May 20, 1983, 119 delegates met in the town hall of Spennymoor to select their candidate. Each nominee gave a short speech and took questions for five minutes. By John Burton's account, Blair, who spoke last, "was brilliant, excellent—energetic and alive with ideas."

The voting was done in rounds. After each vote, one or more of the seven "short list" candidates would drop off, having received the least number of votes. It took five rounds for Blair to emerge the winner, although he led in each round. In the fifth round, Blair came out on top with 73 votes, as compared to his opponent's 46.

It was time to celebrate, although the general election was less than three weeks away. Blair called his wife, who was running for Parliament from the Thanet North district. The campaign roared into high gear with speeches and rallies and appearances. Cherie and her actor father, Tony Booth, also campaigned for Blair. The members of the Sedgefield posse threw themselves into the task of getting their man elected.

On June 9, 1983, they delivered. Blair was elected to the House of Commons by an 8,281-vote majority. Nationally, the Labour Party had done miserably, taking only 28 percent of the vote. Cherie came in third in her race, but in Trimdon, there was rejoicing and planning for the future MP from Sedgefield, Tony Blair.

4

The Labour MP

THE LABOUR PARTY WAS DEEPLY DIVIDED WHEN BLAIR SETTLED INTO HIS new position as the youngest Labour MP. The leftist element still loudly advocated increased public ownership of business, withdrawal from the European Economic Community, and more power for trade unions. Blair was considerably more moderate in his views, although he was savvy enough to toe the party line when necessary.

Blair made a promising start with his first speech to the House of Commons on July 6, 1983. He said that mass unemployment was unacceptable and that without work, his constituents "not only suffer the indignity of enforced idleness—they wonder how they can afford to get married, to start a family, and have access to all the benefits of society that they should be able to take for granted."

Blair also offered a summary of his personal beliefs about socialism. It was an almost old-fashioned expression of

fundamental beliefs that reflected Blair's intensely moral out-
look on life. "I am a socialist not through reading a textbook
that has caught my intellectual fancy, nor through unthink-
ing tradition, but because I believe that at its best, socialism corresponds most closely to an existence that is both
rational and moral."

Blair shared an office with Gordon Brown, another young
politician looking to move up the ladder in the House of
Commons. Brown and Blair were to play important roles in
each other's careers. Brown was somewhat more experienced
politically and generally played the role of senior partner. As
a former television reporter, Brown could use the media better, but Blair had a better feel for how ordinary middle-class
people thought and what those people considered important.
Blair's admiration of Brown kept him satisfied to be student to
Brown's teacher for many years.

Another Labour MP, John Smith, was instrumental in
Blair's and Brown's success. Smith was the new shadow employment secretary, and he recruited Blair and Brown to serve on a
committee to examine a bill introduced by the Conservatives to
reform trade union law.

Shadow cabinet officers are one of several customs observed
in the British House of Commons. The party out of power, also
called the opposition, selects members to act as counterparts
to the government cabinet members and their assistants. These
shadow positions aren't really jobs but rather a way to divide
up the task of keeping an eye on the government. The party
leader awards the top positions, and lower positions are in
turn assigned by the shadow cabinet members. It ensures a
somewhat more efficient way for members of both parties to
cooperate or, more likely, to disagree. About one-third of the
Labour MPs were members of the shadow government.

Another custom involves backbenchers and frontbenchers,
which refers first to the seating arrangement in the Commons
but has other implications. Newcomers to Parliament and

A delegation of Labour MPs, including (from left) Robert Parry, Nicholas Brown, Michael Cocks, Tony Blair, and Ken Weetch, lobbied Chancellor of Exchequer Nigel Lawson about the effect of spiraling taxation on tobacco.

others with little power or ambition are relegated to the back bench. If a member works hard and makes the right political connections, he or she may get promoted to the front bench. Early promotion is quite rare, which is why Blair was stunned when he was offered a move to the front bench after only seventeen months in Parliament. Summoned to see Labour Party leader Neil Kinnock, Blair was nervous, sure that he had done something wrong. The opposite was the case, and Blair moved to the front bench.

He joined the shadow chancellor of the exchequer's team as a junior member. Shadow Chancellor Roy Hattersley was impressed with the young Blair. He said of Blair, "He was just as good as I expected him to be. He was hugely industrious and could always do it. If he had to do hideous things in the House of Commons, like wind up on the third day of the finance bill, he would always do it well."

The chancellor handled treasury duties, so most of the time Blair was called upon to know all there was to know about money policy. One of the big issues then, as now, was integrating monetary policy between Britain and other European countries. Most Labour Party members in 1984 viewed this integration with suspicion. Blair kept to the party line and advised that the timing was wrong.

The Blairs had some changes in their personal lives while Tony was on the rise in Parliament. Their first child, Euan Anthony Blair, was born on January 19, 1984. The couple also bought Myrobella, a rambling old house in the middle of Blair's Sedgefield constituency. The family lived in London during the week but retreated to the country on weekends.

Cherie continued to be active in the Labour Party. She was elected to the executive of the Labour coordinating committee, which provided a moderate voice for modernizing the party. A friend of the Blairs' during the early years said that the couple had an agreement that the first one elected to Parliament would support the other. That may have been true, or perhaps the couple concluded that Tony was better able to get elected and rise farther faster. Eventually, Cherie decided to confine her party influence to a less public one but possibly more powerful as she focused on her family and her law practice. On December 6, 1985, Nicholas was born, and Kathryn followed on March 2, 1988.

BLAIR BUILDS HIS REPUTATION

Blair worked to strengthen his reputation in the House of Commons during this period. His position with the opposition treasury team gave him ample opportunity to speak his views. They were characteristically Labour views, but at least one opponent didn't think those views were heartfelt. Conservative

Tony Blair with his family in San Gimignano, Italy, in 1997. From left to right: Nicky, Cherie, Kathryn, Blair, and Euan.

chancellor Nigel Lawson often matched wits with Blair over monetary policy and free trade. He later expressed the opinion, which was apparently shared by others, that Blair was often just engaging in lawyerly dispute and that there was no deep disagreement: "I was always slightly surprised that he was in the Labour Party at all. He is quite definitely the least socialist leader the Labour Party has ever had."

Three people entered Blair's life during his first term in Parliament who would be extremely influential later in his life.

The first was Alastair Campbell, a journalist who first met Blair in 1983. He later claimed to have seen leadership potential in Blair from the very beginning.

The second person was Peter Mandelson, who was appointed as the Labour Party's director of communications in October 1985. Mandelson was a producer of a British television news show when he took the Labour Party job. He drafted a third person, Philip Gould, to work as a volunteer political consultant. Gould was eager to work in party politics and soon made himself indispensable by doing opinion polling, devising campaign strategies, and creating advertising. This trio, plus Gordon Brown, would be shoulder to shoulder, or they would at least try to give that appearance in the effort to modernize the Labour Party in the person of Tony Blair.

The general election of June 11, 1987 found Labour in much the same position as it had been in 1983. Many of the same issues divided the party and kept the voters loyal to Prime Minister Thatcher. The main difference was the increased sophistication with which the campaign was run. Mandelson deserved much of the credit for the carefully controlled management of television coverage and for the slick ad campaign.

Blair was reelected with an increased majority. The Sedgefield constituency was considered a safe Labour seat so there was never any real doubt that Blair would be returned. Nationally, the Labour Party took another beating with only 31.5 percent of the vote. The party plan had been presented accurately and attractively, but evidently the voters weren't convinced. The Labour Party seemed to have no choice but to institute some major policy changes. It would take several more years and Tony Blair before that could be accomplished.

After the election, Blair made his first try at getting elected to the shadow cabinet. With 15 positions open, Blair came in 17th in the vote. It was a good showing for him and resulted in his appointment to deputy shadow trade and industry secretary. This position was just below the level of the shadow cabinet. It included responsibility for the city of London and consumer affairs, and it offered abundant opportunity to get noticed.

The annual Labour Party conference in September 1987 approved a policy review sought by leader Neil Kinnock. Policy review sounded innocent enough for any party member, left or right, to support. In this instance, however, a review actually meant reframing the Labour Party's most fundamental policies.

Kinnock wanted to restructure three policies: public ownership, trade union law, and defense. Simply put, he wanted to stop the Labour demand for renationalizing industries that the Conservatives had privatized. He wanted trade unions to have less power in almost every area, and he wanted to abandon Labour's position against nuclear weapons.

Blair shared Kinnock's revolutionary ideas, or at least some version of them, from the start. Both men and others around them were skillful politicians and didn't immediately call for party reform. It took many years of maneuvering and compromise for Labour to reshape itself from the inside out.

Blair's year as the deputy shadow trade and industry secretary was a time for him to build support in his party. He wrote regular articles for the *Times*, which gave his fellow MPs a chance to notice him. On November 24, 1987, he advocated television coverage for the House of Commons. "Politics works through publicity and television is the best form of publicity." He attracted some of that publicity himself when he criticized the government for allowing a group of pensioners to lose their life savings through a failure of government regulation. His party rewarded Blair in November 1988 when he was elected to the shadow cabinet. He came in ninth in the voting, while his friend and colleague Gordon Brown came in first. Blair was appointed shadow energy secretary.

The big energy issue in 1988 and 1989 was the impending electricity privatization bill proposed by the Conservatives and opposed by Labour. Blair's handling of the opposition to electricity privatization earned him respect for his ability to identify the key issues for debate and avoid being bogged down in fighting over unimportant aspects of the bill.

Charles Clark, Neil Kinnock's chief of staff during this time, said later of Blair's ability to get to the heart of an issue: "His great skill as a politician is that he has always believed that getting somewhere depended on making the argument. He knows which corner of the room he wants to get to and works out precisely how to get there. Most politicians are never as clear about their destination and, when they are, they find it difficult to find a way around the furniture."

An important part of Labour's opposition centered on nuclear power. The official Labour position was anti–nuclear power. Privately, Blair may not have felt the same way about nuclear power plants as his party did, but he ably defended the party position. At the Labour conference in October 1989, Blair offered the following rhetoric about electricity privatization: "We do not want it postponed, we do not want it delayed, we do not want it put off, we want it abandoned, here, now and forever."

Blair's year as shadow energy secretary was rounded off nicely in November 1989, when the government abandoned the sale of Nuclear Electric. His reward was to come in fourth in the shadow cabinet elections that year. Blair was appointed shadow employment secretary. Blair had earned his promotion, and it meant that he would be squarely in the middle of yet another challenge to modernize the Labour Party. Somehow the relationship between Labour and trade unions had to be changed.

CHAPTER

5

Moving up
the Ladder

BLAIR'S FIRST IMPORTANT JOB AS SHADOW EMPLOYMENT SECRETARY
was to persuade the Labour Party to abandon the policy of
a closed shop. The difficulty lay more in getting the unions
to support this move than in getting the party to accept the
reversal of one of Labour's most traditional positions. A
closed shop meant that all employees in a union-organized
occupation were required to join that union as a condition of
their employment.

This policy had come up for review when the European
Commission released a draft of their social charter that called
for every employer and employee to have the right to join a
union or not without any occupational or personal damage to
be suffered by those people. Labour had supported the charter
because it guaranteed many rights for workers, but this lat-
est draft went much further than the official party stance on
closed shop.

TONY BLAIR DEALT WITH EMPLOYMENT ISSUES SUCH AS MINIMUM WAGE, FULL EMPLOYMENT, AND LABOR UNION LAW CHANGES.

Blair began a speedy recruitment of Labour leaders and union bosses to a new point of view. He used a simple approach by telling them that there was no other way to resolve this issue than to abandon the closed shop. In order to secure the right for all workers to join a union, the opposite right of not joining had to be accepted.

In a week, Blair had obtained the necessary support. Some Labour Party members and union members complained about Blair's bypassing any hint of democratic procedure, but as the Conservatives had been denied one of their best "pointed sticks" to jab at Labour, party members soon recovered. It was around this time, the beginning of 1990, that Blair began a sure-footed rise to the top of his party. Before the closed shop policy scuffle, Blair was relatively unknown in the Labour Party and by the public. That situation began to change as Blair dealt with employment issues such as minimum wage, full employment, and labor union law changes. He didn't prevail with Labour's traditional positions on these issues for the most part, but his efforts raised his party's regard for him. The party and the public started to get the message that the Labour Party must be reformed and modernized. The unspoken message was that Tony Blair was the man for the job.

It didn't hurt Blair's rise that rival Gordon Brown was having his own troubles. As shadow trade and industry secretary, Brown had to deal with some nationalization issues, but he lacked Blair's boldness. Without a doubt, Brown had a better understanding of economic policy than anyone else in his party but tended to plod in his decision making. Perhaps the results were the same, but his style was lacking.

Style was something Blair had in abundance. At the time of the Labour Party conference in 1991, he was being mentioned more and more often as leader material.

TRANSITIONS

During this period, the Conservatives had their troubles. The economic good times of the Thatcher years had been replaced with high interest rates and high unemployment. At the end of 1990, Prime Minister Thatcher was forced to resign. She was replaced by John Major. Major continued the same general policies as Thatcher with the notable exception of abolishing a hated poll tax that Thatcher had placed on property. His less abrasive personality and natural conciliatory ability gave the Conservatives a little bump in the opinion polls.

Major searched for the right time to call the general election but was outflanked by Labour each time as they managed to draw attention to one issue or another that would sway the voters away from the Conservatives. He was almost at the very end of the five-year limit between elections when he called it for April 9, 1992.

The polls suggested that there was some room for optimism among Labour Party members, but Blair apparently didn't share in it. His pessimistic view proved to be correct as Labour received only 35 percent of the vote to the Conservatives' 41.9 percent. Leader Neil Kinnock conceded defeat the following morning. Within hours, the tussle for party leadership began.

The top Labour position was not in question. John Smith was already considered the only choice. The race was for the deputy leadership, and it was hotly contested. Within days after the election, Blair positioned himself for a possible bid for the office.

Tony Blair speaks with former prime minister John Major on May 14, 1997, on the way to the opening of British Parliament. The opening's traditional speech, given by Queen Elizabeth II, outlined the prime minister's program for the next 17 months.

In interviews given right after the election, Blair gave a forthright assessment of the reasons for the defeat. "The true reason for our defeat is not complex. It is simple. It has been the same since 1979. Labour has not been trusted to fulfill the aspirations of the majority of people in a modern world."

The first few days after the 1992 election shaped the party for years to come. Blair may or may not have thought he had a chance to win the deputy leadership post, but he certainly wanted to be in a position to show his preference. There were meetings and phone calls and more meetings and phone calls. Kinnock favored one person for the deputy position, and Smith leaned toward another. Gordon Brown could have contested the head leadership post but didn't because of his long friendship with John Smith. Blair probably could have been deputy to Smith but hesitated since that would have meant vaulting over Brown's head in seniority and likely would have ended their long friendship.

It was a complicated business, but the final result was that John Smith and Margaret Beckett were elected as leader and deputy leader on July 18, 1992. A few days later, Gordon Brown came out on top in the shadow cabinet elections and Blair second. Brown was appointed shadow chancellor of the exchequer, and Blair took over as shadow home secretary. The modernizers were at the helm, excepting John Smith, who was considered a traditionalist.

Blair had wanted the shadow home secretary job. Most politicians calculate the service that will portray them to advantage in the press, and Blair was no exception. Roy Hattersley, the outgoing deputy leader and shadow home secretary, gave his protégé some advice when Blair asked him what he should do. "I told him to take it. It's a rotten job in government. It's a pretty good job in opposition. In government you're waiting for somebody to break out of prison every day. In opposition you're hoping that somebody will break out of prison so you can complain about it."

Hattersley's words confirmed Blair's own belief that working as shadow home secretary had potential for getting a young politician noticed. There was no doubt that Blair was noticed in 1992. This was an important year in his political career. He began to slip slowly out from behind Gordon Brown.

In January 1993, Blair opened a radio interview on *The World This Weekend* with words that continued to echo long after their broadcast. "I think it's important that we are tough on crime and tough on the causes of crime, too." In answer to the interviewer's question about locking up youngsters, Blair agreed that it might sometimes be necessary to do so, although he thought it was more important to deter the crime from the beginning. Blair also agreed that the prison population might

Tony Blair shakes hands with U.S. President Bill Clinton on June 20, 1997. Blair and Clinton were in Denver attending the Summit of the Eight.

rise as a result of this firmness. Blair's statements were decidedly not the answers of traditional Labour.

Blair's thoughts were really brought into focus by a visit he paid to the United States just before his January 10 interview. Blair and Gordon Brown traveled to the United States to visit with President Bill Clinton's winning campaign team. Clinton had just been the first Democrat elected president since 1976. In the past, Democratic Party policies had paralleled many of Labour's views and had suffered the same years in exile from running the government. Clinton won by moving his party closer to the center politically.

Blair saw that Clinton's idea of personal responsibility fit his own views. Clinton believed in assisting welfare recipients with employment training, child care, and medical care but required them to be on their own in two years' time. He also believed in stamping out the roots of crime, but he wasn't afraid to fill up the jails in order to create a safer society. Clinton's viewpoint wasn't the usual Democratic policy and neither was it a Labour view. But if Clinton's success was any measure, it was the people's viewpoint.

The visit seemed to be a turning point for Blair, who found new expression for his long-standing conservative social values. It would always be difficult for a left-wing opposition party to win an election based on tax issues. Traditional left-wing policy usually meant higher taxes in an effort to spread the wealth among all classes of citizens. Blair now saw that it was possible to fight the Conservatives on the basis of social issues, where they were vulnerable.

The visit may have been a wake-up call for Blair, but most of his fellow Labour Party leaders were less excited by the visit. Some of them were downright hostile. They said that the Labour Party was being gutted by this hidden agenda of "Clintonization."

John Smith called Peter Mandelson to his office while Blair and Brown were still in America. According to Mandelson's version, an irritated Smith told him, "All this Clintonization business, it's just upsetting everyone. Stop boat-rocking with all this talk of change and modernization. It will just divide the party. If we remain united, we'll win. Do just shut up."

These were strong words, and Clare Short, an outspoken traditionalist on the Labour Party National Executive Board, had words even stronger. She saw the trip as an attempt by Blair and Brown to sell out the basic values of the party. "The secret, infiltrating so-called modernizers of the Labour Party have been creating myths about why Clinton won, in order to try and reshape the Labour Party in the way they want it to go."

Actually, Smith and Short were fairly accurate in their assessment of Blair and Brown's motives. The pair *was* trying to change the Labour Party, in fundamental ways.

ONE MEMBER, ONE VOTE

A week after launching his "tough on crime" policy, Blair stirred the political waters into a whirlpool when he announced his support for a "one member, one vote" change in the party. At this time, trade unions had block voting privileges within the Labour Party. The trade unions had a certain percentage of votes allotted to them to vote for candidates in a variety of elections within the party. While union members were likely Labour supporters, they did not have to officially join the party and pay dues. The result was that the union leaders had a disproportionate number of votes and thus power in their hands.

Several compromise plans to curtail block voting had been proposed, and some changes were in the works when Blair came out with his plan. It was simple enough. Each party member would be represented by his vote alone. Of course, the unions weren't likely to use their own votes to approve a plan that would give them substantially less power.

Several different plans were proposed in 1993 that were quite a bit less reforming than Blair wanted. Leader John Smith, while convinced that "one member, one vote" was a needed change, was not convinced that 1993 was the time to institute that change

The final compromise was less than Blair and the others wanted but enough of a change to cause quite a fight at the party conference in September 1993. The Labour National Executive had approved a consensus package that allowed one member one vote for parliamentary candidates; changes in the proportions allotted to unions, party members, and MPs in the selection of party leadership; plus cosmetic changes in the block vote at conference.

John Smith staked his leadership post on passing the measure and offered some carrots to the unions by moving in their direction on several issues. One of the moves was a promise made by Smith that would give rights to full-time and part-time workers from "day one" of getting a job. This promise was

British statesman John Smith is pictured at the October 1, 1986, Labour Party Conference in Blackpool, England.

totally at odds with a current policy of protection from unfair dismissal after two years of employment.

In the end, the measure passed when one union decided to abstain. The rule change included some new rules that they judged would conflict with their sex equality policy. The rule change was significant but fell short of Blair's goal of one vote for each member.

Blair gave a telling interview in the *Financial Times* in the fall of 1993. His impatience with John Smith's wait-and-see attitude when it came to significant reform was clear. Blair said, "What I find odd is that after four election defeats and with Labour not having won 40 percent of popular vote since 1970 that you have to argue the case for change."

Smith couldn't have been less than exasperated at Blair's continuing push for change. Smith preferred to let Prime Minister John Major do the work for the Labour Party in this period between elections. The Conservatives still had plenty of problems, and their failure to provide solutions could only help Labour. Why ask for trouble?

Blair found the first few months of 1994 to be frustrating ones. He had less access to the leadership than when Neil Kinnock was leader and consequently was somewhat isolated. Friends said later that by April, Blair was gloomy about his chances as well as the Labour Party chances of ever getting back in power.

Then tragedy struck: John Smith had a heart attack and died on May 12, 1994.

6

Labour Party Leader

TONY BLAIR WAS IN A CAR ON THE WAY TO A ROUTINE PARTY SPEAKING engagement in Aberdeen when news came of John Smith's heart attack. A series of phone calls confirmed the shocking news: Smith was dead. Blair went on with his engagements as planned but did make a short statement to the media, in which he spoke of Smith. "He had this extraordinary combination of strength and authority and humour and humanity, and all of us who knew him closely, personally, will mourn him."

Blair took an early flight back to London alone and probably for the first time that day was able to think about what this might mean to his own political aspirations. There's no doubt that Blair genuinely grieved the loss of his friend and boss, but politics would pause only briefly to honor Smith. Realistically, Blair had to make some quick decisions. It's hard to imagine that his decision to run for leader wasn't made on that solitary flight back home.

Even as the press eulogized John Smith, they speculated on the identity of the next Labour leader. Within hours of Smith's death, Blair had been named the front-runner. Blair's supporters turned up at his office even before he returned from Aberdeen. He listened to them but made no commitment. It would be several days before he officially announced his candidacy.

The greatest obstacle to Blair's running was Gordon Brown. Since the very beginning of their friendship, there had been a mostly unspoken agreement that Brown would run for the top leadership spot if the opportunity arose, and Tony would support him. The last time this agreement had played much of a role was in 1992. Two years later, much had changed, but it was soon obvious that Brown didn't see it that way.

Blair had finally pulled ahead of his political big brother in those two years. He had had a successful run as shadow home secretary and had gained visibility in the party and among the general public. Before he died, John Smith had predicted Blair would succeed him.

Gordon Brown did not give up his big opportunity without a fight, although it was done privately in meetings with Blair and other leaders. Finally he was forced to concede that while he might have some advantage among party MPs, Blair was much more likely to be able to win for Labour in the next general election. It was a bitter pill for Brown to swallow.

One added element of tension in the decision was the involvement of Peter Mandelson. Now an MP and former director of communications for the Labour Party, Mandelson was a friend to both Blair and Brown. He had led Brown to believe that his first loyalty when it came to the leadership was Brown. That was probably true until after Smith's death and the subsequent overwhelming interest in Blair. Mandelson thought Blair could win the general election and waffled on his support for Brown at a crucial moment. The friendship was fractured,

Blair congratulates Shadow Chancellor Gordon Brown after a speech at the Labour Party's annual conference in October 1995. Blair and Brown have had a competitive yet supportive working relationship.

and Mandelson and Brown would give Blair many headaches over the next few years.

Officially the campaign for Labour Party leader started on June 10, 1994, and concluded on July 21 when Blair was elected. At 41, Blair was the youngest party leader ever elected and probably the least traditional leader as well. In his acceptance speech at the Institute of London, Blair issued a call. "I say this to the people of this country, and most of all to our young people: join us in this crusade for change."

The summer of 1994 found Blair on a working holiday in France, where he planned his first Labour conference as leader. He wanted his first conference to be seen as a decisive break from the past. He had convinced Alastair Campbell to take the job of press secretary. Campbell's first task was to sell the Labour Party on dumping Clause IV of its constitution.

FIGHTING CLAUSE IV

Drafted in 1917, Clause IV was considered out of date almost before the first Labour government took office several years later. It was a very strong statement of traditional socialistic belief:

> To secure for the workers by hand or by brain the full fruits of their industry and the most equitable distribution thereof that may be possible upon the basis of the common ownership of the means of production, distribution and exchange, and the best obtainable system of popular administration and control of each industry or service.

The modern Labour Party wanted more public ownership and an economic system that was different from capitalism, but common ownership was no longer sought. Clause IV was a symbol more than a tenet of the Labour Party. Fresh from his victory, Blair thought now was the time to symbolically bring the Labour Party closer to middle-class British citizens.

Blair's attempt to abolish Clause IV was not the first. Leaders had tried for over 30 years to change or get rid it. Neil Kinnock and John Smith agreed, but neither thought the timing was right.

The new Labour leader was up for the fight. It was the first shot in his battle to win the next general election. He expected that the party would disagree while speaking of historical tradition, and they did. However, Blair gambled that they wanted to win the next election more than they wanted to preserve a statement drafted over seventy years previously.

Blair announced his intention to rewrite Clause IV at the party conference in October of 1994, and the fight began. In December 1994, the Labour National Executive agreed to call a special party conference in the spring of 1995 to consider the constitutional change.

THE SCHOOLING CONTROVERSY

December also brought another event that was potentially more damaging to Blair than any of his prior political decisions. The Blairs confirmed in December that they would be sending their 10-year-old son, Euan, to the London Oratory, a state-funded Roman Catholic boys' school. The school was required to accept children regardless of ability or background apart from religion. The trouble arose because the Oratory had taken advantage of a conservative law allowing it to opt out of local school council control. The school could interview students before accepting them, supposedly to assess their "religious suitability" for the school. Although not the official intent, that process could allow the school to choose students based on ability.

The Labour Party was firmly opposed to any hint of class favoritism in schools and wanted to abolish such institutions as the London Oratory altogether. Blair's fellow party members thought he should set a better example, or at least that was the thrust of the uproar created over Euan's new school.

Blair didn't back down. He simply said, "I am not going to make a choice for my child on the basis of what is the politically correct thing to do." He sought to refocus attention by proposing immediate measures to raise school standards and help failing institutions. Eventually, the uproar died down, and Euan was off to school. The school argument would never have taken on the importance it did had it not raised lingering anxieties among Labour Party members that Tony Blair was attempting to abandon their basic values.

Anxiety drained away in the spring, when Blair began a tour to meet party members. He held question and answer sessions all over the country and was a hit with the people who might have doubted him in the beginning.

The new Clause IV was approved by a 65 percent vote at the April meeting. It was a rather vague statement that came to characterize New Labour. It argued strongly for strength in community but didn't mention common ownership.

The victorious Blair spoke briefly after the result was announced. "I wasn't born into this party. I chose it. I've never joined another political party. I believe in it. I'm proud to be the leader of it and it's the party I'll always live in and I'll die in." Loud applause greeted his words.

With the Clause IV battle won, Blair settled down for the long haul before the general election. Increasingly, the polls indicated that Labour could expect to win due in great measure to the troubles the Conservative government continued to have. Britain's economic woes still lingered along with dissention in the Conservative Party over membership in the European Union (EU). There was a near rebellion in the party over adopting the single currency that the EU advocated.

The months before the election didn't have any huge political crises for Blair, but they did have their share of political tension. The feud between Gordon Brown and Peter Mandelson heated up until Blair often had to placate one or the other. An emotional Mandelson repeatedly showed his displeasure regarding his unofficial job in the campaign. Blair reassured Mandelson of his vital role as political advisor and coach, but Mandelson seemed unable to believe his boss and friend.

It didn't help that Brown was also essential to the campaign, and Mandelson knew it. Brown may have felt cheated at being denied the party leadership, but he wanted Blair to win the election.

The annual Labour Party Conference held in October 1995 went smoothly for Blair. With no big issues to distract attention from his drive toward election, Blair used his conference address to further set out his vision. "It is a moral purpose to life, a set of values, and a belief in society, in cooperation. We aren't simply people set in isolation from each other, face to face with eternity, but members of the same family, community, the same human race. This is my socialism."

The most serious and only real crisis of Blair's years of Labour Party leadership came over yet another school-related decision. Just before Christmas 1995, Harriet Harman, shadow health secretary, told Blair of her decision to send her son to a selective grammar school. One of 160 selective state schools, St. Olave's made no pretense of having open admission policies. While Blair was irritated with Harman for her choice, he could hardly condemn her for a decision that she thought was best for her child. The controversy over Euan's schooling had taken place only a year earlier. In the end, no lasting damage was done politically to Blair.

The next year was a buildup to the election. Prime Minister Major could have called an election any time in that year, so preparation had to be ongoing. Blair and his team laid the foundation for popular support in several areas.

In a distinctly un-Labour position, Blair called for no direct tax increase even among upper income earners. Chancellor Brown wanted to leave open the possibility of raising the tax rate on very high incomes, but in the end he was overruled. Blair thought the time had come to disassociate the Labour Party from its past support for increased taxes. Labour and higher taxes for increased spending on social programs had long been synonymous. Blair judged this to be the time to change that perception.

Blair also took steps to bring the Liberals, a minority political party, into the fold. Labour needed what was known as a "Lib-Lab coalition," just in case it should fail to gain a clear majority in Parliament. The Labour Party appeared to be heading for a landslide victory, but Blair was taking no chances.

Blair and his campaign team seemed unduly pessimistic about Labour's chances of winning the general election. In

Blair addresses the Labour conference of October 1995. In his keynote speech, Blair pledged that the national railway network, scheduled to be privatized by the Conservative government, would remain in public hands under a future Labour government. He also alluded to his belief in the "moral purpose" of life.

spite of polls, focus groups, and canvassing that predicted a Labour success, Blair and his cohorts seemed to need the psychological advantage of fighting a hard battle. It was probably foremost in their minds that a Labour victory had also been predicted in 1992 and didn't materialize.

John Major asked the queen to dissolve Parliament on March 17, 1997. May 1 was set for the general election. The Blair campaign was set to go with a flurry of interviews and appearances. The Blair Battle Buses took to the road on April 1. Tony Blair traveled from stop to stop with basically the same message as he told his Northampton audience the first day. "It's a beautiful day. The sun is out and with a bit of luck and your support the Tories'll be out too."

Like most modern campaigns, the 1997 one was fought hardest in offices and television studios. The role of the media could hardly be overstated. Blair took a cautious approach to virtually any hint of radical change. The Labour manifesto, or party platform, was launched on April 3. Education was called the highest priority, and there was a promise not to raise income taxes. There was little to suggest that the traditional Labour Party even still existed.

THE ELECTION

On May 1, 1997, Tony and Cherie were at their home, Myrobella, in Sedgefield. As evening approached, exit polls predicted a landslide vote for Blair. The polls closed at 10:00 P.M., and exit numbers finally gave over to early results with the same good news. Blair later spoke of that evening: "Realising that you are about to become Prime Minister is a very strange moment. My dad was fabulous. He was absolutely knocked out by it. He said: 'Mum would have been very proud.' But he read my mood correctly. He kept saying to me during the evening: 'You will do it well.' He understood what I was worrying about."

John Major called to concede defeat, and President Clinton called to congratulate Blair. By early morning, Blair and his entourage were on their way back to London. The sky was just lightening as Tony and Cherie made their way to the platform at the Royal Festival Hall where the election night party was being held. When the excited tumult had subsided, Blair spoke, "A new dawn has broken, has it not?"

Tony Blair was just four days from his forty-fourth birthday when he became prime minister. In 14 years, he had risen from unknown barrister to a major player on the world stage.

CHAPTER

7

Prime Minister Blair

IN GREAT BRITAIN, PRIME MINISTERS TAKE OVER IMMEDIATELY AFTER THE
results of the election are known. Therefore, Blair met with
Queen Elizabeth on May 2 after only a few hours of sleep. As is
the custom, the queen asked Blair to form a new administra-
tion of government. Prime Minister Blair arrived at Number
10 Downing Street, the official residence, at 1:00 P.M. He gave
the traditional remarks from the front steps and followed his
children in through the big black door.

Blair had only been in the Downing Street home once
before and talked later about his second trip. He described
walking down the corridor to a little room just off the cabinet
room, where the cabinet secretary, Sir Robin Butler, greeted
him with the words, "Well you're in charge. What are we going
to do, then?"

The British parliamentary system mandates a quick tran-
sition when the party in control changes. This is possible in

part because of the large group of civil service or permanent government employees, which carry over from one government to the next. The prime minister appoints his cabinet and ministers from his fellow members of Parliament. Most of the other positions are filled on a permanent and non-partisan basis. As early as 18 months before the election, some of Blair's staff had met with permanent secretaries to talk about logistics should a handover of government be necessary. The result was a smooth change of government, with the new prime minister able to name his cabinet and ministers within three or four days. The moving van made two trips to the Blairs' London home on Monday to gather up the belongings that would be moved to Downing Street. The official residence wasn't as big as their home, so many things had to be left behind. Eventually, the Blairs sold their London home and sent the rest of their furnishings to Myrobella.

Traditionally, the chancellor of the exchequer lived in a flat or apartment over Numbers 11 and 12 Downing Street. Secret planning before the election led to the agreement that, if elected, the Blairs would live in the larger flat over 11 and 12, and Gordon Brown would live over Number 10. It was the first time in decades that a prime minister had young children. Blair's three children were aged 13, 11, and 9 years when they moved in.

By Tuesday, May 6, the Blairs were moved in, and the new Labour government had announced its first major policy decision. Chancellor Gordon Brown raised interest rates a quarter point and announced that in the future the Bank of England would handle all such decisions on interest rates. The bank was mandated to change interest rates as necessary to control inflation and promote the economic growth and stability of the country.

It was an unexpected change and enthusiastically greeted by the economic community. It brought home the fact that a new face was living at Number 10, and a new party was in the

Cherie and Tony Blair assume their residence at 10 Downing Street on May 2, 1997. Blair won the election by a landslide, leaving the Conservative Party with its poorest election results since 1832.

majority. The grumblers might mention that this move hadn't been approved by the Labour Party or, for that matter, by the new cabinet, which hadn't even met yet when Brown issued his news. Any disagreement was put aside in the thrill of Labour's finally being back in government. Blair's first months in office were busy ones as he flew from one country to another for meetings. There was little to mar his introduction to the world, and if opinion polls were true, Blair's own countrymen were quite proud that they had shown the good sense to elect him.

At the end of August 1997 came the death of Princess Diana and a further firming of Blair's popularity. His deft handling of the difficult time helped extend the traditional "honeymoon" period for new leaders by a couple of months.

The British people had been at odds with their royal family for some time. The younger generation's failed marriages and often outrageous behavior had begun to make abolishing the monarchy seem like a good idea. Diana, however, had the sympathy of most Britons. They saw her as a victim of the royal family's firm adherence to the old ways. They admired her in spite of her occasional public outbursts. Perhaps she was a bit unstable emotionally, but that only strengthened the public's conviction that at heart she was like them. Blair had been spending the weekend at his home in Trimdon. The phone awakened him in the early morning with news that Diana, Princess of Wales, had been seriously injured in a car accident in Paris. At 3:30 A.M., the telephone brought the news that Diana, her boyfriend Dodi Fayed, and their driver all were dead.

Alastair Campbell phoned next to discuss the appropriate response. Blair believed that the public's grief over the terrible accident would be monumental. He also agreed with Campbell that the public would see this as a test for the new prime minister.

Blair was scheduled to attend church in nearby Sedgefield later that morning. He knew that the television cameras would be there, expecting him to make a statement. Most of his staff had gone back to London for the weekend, so Blair called local friend and fellow party member Phil Wilson for help with the media. Wilson sped to the Blair home, bringing a black necktie just in case Blair didn't have one at his country house.

By the time Blair arrived at St. Mary's church in his borrowed necktie, he was ready to speak to the nation about the terrible news from Paris. The usually stoic Britons felt as if their hearts were broken, and the prime minister joined them in their grief:

> I feel like everyone else in this country today. I am utterly devastated. . . . People everywhere, not just here in Britain, kept faith with Princess Diana. They liked her, they loved her, and they regarded her as one of the people. She was the people's princess, and that is how she will stay, how she will remain in our hearts and our memories forever.

In the following days, Blair unobtrusively guided the royal family in planning a funeral fit for the "people's princess." Diana's family, the Spencers, wanted a private funeral. The queen would have allowed that, but Prime Minister Blair, with the support of Prince Charles, persuaded her that a public funeral was necessary. A special room was set up in Buckingham Palace in the week between Diana's death and her funeral to coordinate plans. Daily planning meetings were held, with some of Blair's staff in attendance to help with organization.

Blair was at the Northolt Royal Air Force base when Princess Diana's body was flown back from France. When the queen was attacked in the tabloid newspapers for not showing enough public grief, Blair defended her by saying that the royal family shared "our" grief over Diana's death. He advised the queen to lower the flag over Buckingham Palace to half-mast, an American custom, to help silence the tabloid newspapers that daily proclaimed the queen's great insensitivity. He suggested lengthening the funeral procession route and broadcasting the funeral service over loudspeakers outside Westminster Abbey.

The funeral brought forth an outpouring of emotion; the traditionally "stiff upper lip" Britons unusually expressed their emotions in public. Along with many others, Prime Minister Blair led a reading from the Bible: 1 Corinthians 13. In the days after the funeral, it became apparent that Blair had helped the queen and Prince Charles through a dangerous interlude in which the public could see the royals only as Diana's oppressors. Blair's intervention softened the public perception of the royals and made the family appear closer to its subjects.

Blair had emerged as a bright spot. His direct style and articulate manner were called a breath of fresh air. The new prime minister had been tested and found to be solid but sensitive. It was a combination that held very wide appeal.

THE FIRST CRISIS

The first policy crisis of Blair's term came in the fall and was labeled the "Ecclestone affair." One of the Labour Party's manifesto items was the promise to ban tobacco advertising. An aspect of this policy was to ban tobacco companies from sponsoring race cars. The ban had been expected to be somewhere off in the future, but pressure from the EU threatened to push the tobacco ban forward with immediate enforcement.

This was not good news to the Formula 1 racing executives who requested a meeting with Prime Minister Blair. The meeting itself might not have mattered had not the Labour Party previously accepted a donation of £1 million from Bernie Ecclestone, one of the Formula 1 executives.

The donation came about six months after Blair and his family had been treated to a special day at the Silverstone track, home of Formula 1. Blair and the children took a run around the track with one of Britain's most well-known racecar drivers. Later, Blair met with Ecclestone and other movers and shakers in the race car world in a trackside mobile home. It wasn't an unusual outing for a politician, but Blair evidently saw no reason to register the visit with the Register of Members' Interests, as required. In January 1997, Ecclestone made his donation to the Labour Party.

It appeared that Ecclestone's meeting with Blair in October 1997 had triggered a direct response when Blair asked that a way be found to protect the interests of sports in general and Formula 1 in particular. By the beginning of November, the press had discovered the meeting between Blair and Ecclestone and the donation made earlier. With charges of a conflict of interest flying, Blair and his associates struggled in typical political fashion to minimize the damage. Finally, they returned the donation, and Blair apologized publicly for his handling of the affair. He stuck to his story that he hadn't traded influence for money, but he said that he could understand that the appearance of wrongdoing existed. In the end, he counted on citizens to give a new leader the benefit of the doubt, which they did, allowing him to scrape through his first crisis as prime minister.

The next crisis, although far less important, was probably more aggravating to Blair. In January 1998, a biography of Gordon Brown was released early and caused an immediate uproar. The book revealed that its subject and his followers believed that Blair had cheated Chancellor Brown of the premiership.

Brown had already annoyed Blair and Campbell with some petty incidents of wrong choices. Brown seemed unable or unwilling to conceal his brooding ambitious nature and refused to get rid of his press officer, Charlie Whelan, who appeared to lead his boss into mischief. Brown tried unsuccessfully to distance himself from the biography written by Paul Routledge. He had agreed to at least one interview with the author and had allowed Whelan and other staff members to work closely with Routledge.

Evidently, Blair and Campbell thought the biography fuss indicated a need to bring Brown up short, although probably not with as much of a yank as ensued. A newspaper columnist reported that a "senior source inside Downing Street" said it was time for Brown to get a grip on his "psychological flaws." It's doubtful that Blair intended such a phrase to be reported publicly, although it must have reflected his views. Blair immediately went into reverse spin by praising Brown for his intellectual powers. Blair needed Brown for his grasp of economic issues, but he must have felt weary from trying to get on with the prickly chancellor.

THE CONTINUING CONFLICT IN NORTHERN IRELAND

In the spring of 1998, another thorny issue took center stage. Much progress had already been made to end the conflict in Northern Ireland, but the time was at hand for a breakthrough. Former prime minister John Major had worked doggedly at getting the fighting parties to the negotiation table. His insistence that the Irish Republican Army (IRA) must lay down its arms before joining the peace talks was a snagging point. The IRA, represented by its political arm, Sinn Féin, refused to disarm until they were permitted to join the talks.

Within two weeks of his election, Tony Blair made a trip to Northern Ireland to show his support. The demand for IRA disarmament before talks started was dropped. In September 1997, contacts began between the two governments and eight parties concerned. By March 1998, George Mitchell, a retired U.S. senator who was in charge of the talks, told Blair that he thought an agreement was in sight.

Blair made the risky decision to announce a deadline for an agreement. In a news conference on March 25, he set a deadline of April 9 and flew to Belfast, Northern Ireland, on April 7. His very presence for the talks put pressure on the participants to buckle down and negotiate a compromise. No party wanted to be blamed for the failure of the peace talks. Blair and the others met in Castle Buildings on the grounds of Stormont, Belfast. In short sleeves, often with his feet propped up on the table, Blair helped draft version after version of the agreement. In the late afternoon of April 10, 1998, Blair and Irish prime minister Bertie Ahern announced the agreement, which would become known as the Good Friday Agreement. The agreement said that Northern Ireland would remain part of the United Kingdom as long as the majority wished it and that there would be a sharing of power with Sinn Féin. Ireland would give up its claim to a united Ireland, and Northern Ireland would return to self-government. It was understood that the IRA would begin the process of disarming, although no deadline was set for that process to commence. No party considered it an ideal agreement, but nonetheless it was a historical moment.

Referendums in Ireland and Northern Ireland were scheduled immediately, and by the end of May, the agreement had been approved. In June, an election was held to select representatives to the Northern Ireland Assembly. In November 1998, Blair spoke to the Irish Dáil, the lower house of the Irish parliament, in Dublin. He was the first British prime minister ever to speak to that body.

In his speech, Blair illustrated his ability to look at the basic issues in any situation. "It is all about belonging. The wish of Unionists is to belong to the U.K. The wish of Nationalists is to belong to Ireland. Both traditions are reasonable. There are no absolutes. The beginning of understanding is to realize that."

Throughout this time and on into the next year, Blair was working on other issues of reform. A deal was made with the House of Lords, the other body of Parliament, whose members served by right of heredity. This deal abolished most of the hereditary seats. Home rule for Scotland and Wales was instituted, and Blair promoted his "Third Way" concept throughout Europe and the United States.

First used as a description for Blair's economic plans, the "Third Way" came to stand for a modernized social democracy. It more or less advocated taking the middle ground on such issues as privatization of industries and nationalization of the same. Blair expanded the meaning to include all modernization and reform plans. Even though Blair said it wasn't simply a centrist policy, members of both the far right and far left of his party never saw it in any other way.

U.S. president Bill Clinton found the "Third Way" to be an apt description for much of his policies. Clinton and his

Irish Prime Minster Bertie Ahern and British Prime Minister Tony Blair shake hands at the end of the Northern Ireland Peace Talks in Belfast on April 10, 1998. The Good Friday Agreement heralded a new era in the governance of British-ruled Northern Ireland.

wife, Hillary, attended meetings and held a couple of seminars with Blair on the subject. Blair's much-discussed friendship with Clinton was based in large measure on their many similar views. Blair had taken many political pages from Clinton's election book and thought Clinton was brilliant, with a quick grasp of relevant detail.

The two leaders would become closer over the next few years, and the friendship prospered even after Clinton finished his second term and returned to private life.

December 1998 was a busy month for Prime Minister Blair. On December 16, he announced that British armed forces would join the United States in launching air strikes against Iraq. Iraqi leader Saddam Hussein continued to defy United Nations (UN) orders issued after the Gulf War in 1991. The call to action seemed clear: Iraq had to bow to international pressure or suffer the consequences.

In the midst of this crisis, Alastair Campbell brought unwelcome news of a different sort to Blair. The newspapers were about to break a story that would put Peter Mandelson in a bad spot. Mandelson had been appointed secretary for trade and industry in July 1998 in a cabinet reshuffle. The newspapers were about to report that Mandelson had accepted a loan of £373,000 from a fellow MP who was now in the ministry. The loan was used to buy Mandelson's house in Notting Hill, a fashionable neighborhood in London, in 1996. The loan gave the appearance of affecting Mandelson's advice about ministerial appointments after the election.

There was never any proof that the loan was improper, but Mandelson had to go. He resigned his cabinet position on December 23. The biggest question was how the press came to find out about the loan. The route seemed to lead back to the feud between Chancellor Brown and Mandelson. It's doubtful that Brown himself had any part, but one of his overzealous followers may have decided to bring down the enemy Mandelson.

The last year of the twentieth century was dawning, and Blair must have been hoping that 1999 would begin more smoothly than 1998 had finished.

8

The Negotiator

A PARTY CELEBRATING THE LAUNCH OF THE EURO WAS MISSING A significant guest on December 31, 1998. Eleven of the fifteen nations of the EU would begin 1999 by locking their currencies together. The actual notes and coins wouldn't be used for three more years, but in trading on the exchange markets, the euro replaced all existing currencies of the eleven countries.

Britain was not one of the eleven. Relationships with Europe had long been a bone of contention in Britain. For many years, Britain had scorned the idea of joining with Europe in any way and only joined the European Economic Community in 1973. The idea of abandoning Britain's national currency, the pound, was far from popular.

Blair had always been pro-Europe in his views because he was a multilateralist. Perhaps the lessons he had learned about community from John Macmurray's writings in college influenced him in his determination that Britain should stand

Tony Blair had watched the situation worsen in Kosovo for over a year but had been unable to do more than issue strong warnings to Milosevic.

together with the rest of Europe. However, he had grown progressively quieter on the subject of the single currency as the 1997 election approached. It wasn't that he wanted to get rid of the pound but rather that he saw its demise as inevitable. Britain was yoked with Europe whether the country liked it or not. Blair opted to let the issue rest while he measured public opinion over a period of months, but by 1999, that opinion was more set against the euro than it had ever been. So the launch party for the euro went on without Britain.

A much more deadly problem was looming in the Balkans, a collection of small countries in southeastern Europe, which had long been a hotbed of volatile nationalistic feelings. The Yugoslav federation had broken up in 1991, leaving ethnic warlords fighting among themselves. Primary among the aggressors was Slobodan Milosevic, leader of Serbia. Milosevic had been stopped once, in Bosnia in 1995, where he had carried out what amounted to an "ethnic cleansing," or genocide. Finally, the North Atlantic Treaty Organization (NATO) had ordered air strikes along with ground artillery, causing Milosevic to agree to peace talks.

The winter of 1999 found Milosevic once again embarking on ethnic cleansing, this time in Kosovo, which had been an autonomous province of Serbia. Milosevic had declared martial law and was undertaking a brutal oppression of the Albanian Muslims who had always made Kosovo their home.

Great Britain and the United States wanted no part of more military action in the Balkans. The United States, led by Clinton, had reluctantly joined in the operation in Bosnia in 1995, and Britain, under John Major, had been almost as reluctant. Neither leader thought they could maintain support in their own countries if there was any suggestion that ground troops might be needed to suppress the Serbs.

The situation was much the same in 1999, with one exception: Tony Blair was now prime minister. He had watched the situation worsen in Kosovo for over a year but had been unable to do more than issue strong warnings to Milosevic. The UN and NATO were both cool to the idea of air strikes against Serbia. The UN knew Russia would veto any action, and NATO leaders didn't think their own citizens would support any move that might involve ground troops.

Blair took every occasion possible in 1998 and early 1999 to persuade other countries to act—and soon. The violence escalated until NATO finally approved air strikes in October 1998. They weren't carried out, as Milosevic immediately backed down. After a short cease-fire, a brutal massacre occurred at Racak in Kosovo: a fleeing group of 45 people were shot and hacked to death by Serbian Interior Ministry police on January 15, 1999.

In the days that followed, there were threats and talks and stalling until finally the air strikes were ordered and began on March 24, 1999. Initially, the NATO commanders were greatly restricted in the targets they could attack in an effort to prevent casualties. The first effect of the bombing was a huge flood of Kosovo refugees pouring over the borders with Macedonia and Albania. It appeared that Milosevic had simply expelled hundreds of thousands of Kosovar Albanians.

The magnitude of the exodus from Kosovo in response to the bombing was unexpected to the NATO allies, but they responded quickly to the crisis by setting up refugee camps to house the people.

Blair worked unceasingly throughout this time to convince the NATO allies that ground forces should at least be an option on the table. From the beginning of the air strikes, the NATO commanders were forbidden to even plan a ground assault. President Clinton was the most important opposition. He thought he couldn't keep the support of the American people and the U.S. Congress if escalation was a possibility.

Blair, on the other hand, approved the use of ground troops from the start. It was certainly not the position of the Labour government or the Conservative opposition. The usually politically cautious Blair seemed not to care about any political fallout from his views. His language only toughened as the bombing campaign continued. In a 1999 newspaper article in the *London Sun,* he stated, "This is now a battle of good against evil . . . It is a battle between civilisation and barbarity, democracy against dictatorship."

Blair continued his lobbying efforts among fellow NATO members with some success, in that the approved targets for bombing were expanded. Permission for ground troops was still withheld, but NATO secretary general Javier Solana did finally agree to review the military options. On April 22, 1999, in Chicago, Blair gave an important speech in his personal campaign to influence American public opinion toward a stronger stand in Kosovo. He agreed that a policy of nonintervention in other countries' affairs was a valid one, but he also said, "Acts of genocide can never be a purely internal matter."

On May 3, Blair and his wife visited a refugee camp in Macedonia. The people chanted, "Tony, Tony." He responded, "Our commitment to defeating this policy of ethnic cleansing, our commitment to allowing these people to return to their homes in peace—that commitment is total . . . This is not a battle for NATO, this is not a battle for territory; this is a battle for humanity, it is a just cause, it is a rightful cause."

Near the end of May, envoys from Russia and the EU sensed that Milosevic was searching for a way to retreat. Clinton immediately agreed to send more troops to Kosovo's borders. On May 25, NATO approved the sending of 50,000 soldiers to the region. Blair offered his own description of the change in

Tony Blair greets British soldiers at the Petroved NATO base near Skopje, Macedonia, on May 3, 1999. Blair was at the base to assess the refugee camps near Skopje. In his speech, Blair affirmed his commitment to ending "ethnic cleansing."

policy. "It is important to ensure that we have sufficient ground forces—we will need them on any basis—to do the job of getting the refugees back home."

Clinton then followed up with the announcement that he would be meeting with his military advisors to discuss additional steps, including ground troops. Milosevic's bluff ran out, and he agreed to NATO's demands. On June 10, 1999, the Serbs began to withdraw, and the bombing was halted.

Blair was hailed as a hero in the British press, but his own reaction was far from celebratory as can be shown by his remarks on the steps of Downing Street. "We began this air campaign with reluctance but resolve. We end it with no sense of rejoicing."

Even as the Kosovo conflict was going on, the Good Friday Agreement in Northern Ireland was showing cracks. It seemed to come down to the fact that the Unionists, led by David Trimble, and the IRA/Sinn Féin, led by Gerry Adams, could not agree on the timing of the IRA's disarmament. The Unionists wanted the IRA to disarm before they were allowed to join the Northern Ireland government or at least to disarm at the same time. Sinn Féin would promise nothing without first being allowed to participate in the government.

Blair tried to get the Unionists and Sinn Féin to bridge the gap that separated them, but several sets of talks produced no real agreement. Finally, the talks were suspended in July 1999. In October, Peter Mandelson returned to the cabinet as Northern Ireland secretary. Mandelson had been out for only ten months, but Blair had decided to distance himself from the negotiations, which had taken up so much of his time and energy. Who was better than his old friend Mandelson to stand in for him?

The talks began again a few days after Mandelson took over. There was no immediate and dramatic progress, but the feeling was there that some sort of solution was near. The talks went on throughout November, and finally David Trimble got a yes vote from his party's ruling body, the Ulster Unionist Council, on November 27, 1999. Trimble had to promise to withdraw from the power-sharing government if there was no progress in disarming the IRA by February 2000.

The Unionist vote allowed the sequence of events planned in the Good Friday Agreement to begin immediately. At midnight on November 30, the power of government was officially passed

Sinn Féin demonstrators picket outside the headquarters of the Ulster Unionist Party (UUP) in Belfast on February 11, 2000, protesting the hardline stance the UUP has taken over the lack of progress on decommissioning the IRA. On the same day, Peter Mandelson suspended the powers of the Northern Ireland Assembly.

from the United Kingdom Parliament to the new Northern Ireland Assembly.

The new government ran smoothly enough, but the IRA stalled on the specifics of disarmament, or decommissioning, as they liked to call it. February came, and Trimble had to deliver on his pledge to withdraw from the Northern Ireland Assembly if no progress had been made. Mandelson stepped in instead to suspend the assembly and restore direct rule from Westminster on February 11, 2000. This avoided the appearance that one side or the other had caused the suspension. This setback in February focused attention and mobilized opinion, making the meeting of the May 2000 deadline for a devolved government for Northern Ireland and decommissioning of IRA arms once more a possibility.

On May 6, the IRA announced that it would begin to collect arms and take them to arms dumps, which would be open for an independent inspection. This concession was enough to turn the tide, and on May 30, the Northern Ireland Assembly resumed self-government.

The Northern Ireland talks took up much of the national attention at the time, but the fall of 1999 and the winter of 2000 brought other events. The coming of the millennium did not turn out to be the glorious celebration that had been planned for with great anticipation. It probably would have been impossible for any event to live up to all the hype. The Millennium Dome built in Greenwich was proof of that.

The beginnings of the Millennium Dome project occurred while Blair was still in opposition, but he offered no real resistance to the plans. After he became prime minister, he continued to support funding for the dome although the majority of his cabinet most emphatically didn't agree. The idea to build something to symbolize the coming of a new era was a reasonable one. It was in the execution of that idea that things went awry.

The Millennium Dome was way over budget from the beginning and ended up costing £750 million. Although it had respectable attendance, the visitors never came in the projected numbers. It turned out to be a good science fair but not the overblown beacon to a new century that had been touted.

The spring of 2000 brought further troubles for Blair. None of them were important by themselves but combined seemed to knock him out of step for a short time. The Labour plan to elect the mayor of London directly turned into a disaster when the voters failed to vote the way Labour wanted and elected Ken Livingstone. Blair had strongly opposed Livingstone's election and then had to work with him when Livingstone was elected.

The media played a key role in Blair's perception of himself as out of touch with ordinary voters. They ran stories pointing out that New Labour was not delivering on the very issues they had professed to be at the heart of their manifesto to the voters. Those issues were the family, asylum seekers, crime, and defense. Blair had not yet effectively dealt with many aspects of these issues, and the media was quick to point that out. It was a shaky time for Blair, who had always been able to judge public opinion and govern by it.

Things began to look up a little when the fourth Blair child was born, on May 20, 2000. Leo was the first child born to a serving prime minister since 1849. Blair took a few weeks off to go with Cherie and Leo to the country to help get the baby off to a good start.

It took a different kind of parental trial to pull Blair out of the voter doldrums. On July 6, 2000, Euan Blair, then 16-years-old, was arrested in London's Leicester Square for drunkenness. Apparently, the young man had been celebrating the end of exams and found himself in the hands of the law. It was a scene that many other parents had faced themselves. Blair was embarrassed but supportive of his son. The simple knowledge that even children of prime ministers don't always do what their parents want was enough to bring Blair closer to the people once again.

CHAPTER

9

The World Leader

SEPTEMBER 2000 BROUGHT A NEW SET OF PROBLEMS. PROTESTERS
managed to bring the whole country to a standstill by picket-
ing refineries that delivered fuel to gas stations. Fuel taxes had
risen along with prices until the cost of gas was extremely high.
The protesters were a small group of self-employed truckers
who were probably surprised themselves at the success of their
picket lines. The truck drivers turned away when confronted by
the picketers at the refinery gates. The subsequent run on gas
stations by the public emptied tanks within a little more than
48 hours.

Blair's first instinct was to order troops to drive the gas
trucks, but his advisors convinced him to let the protest die
on its own. After a couple days, the argument for continuing essential public services began to win, and the gas flowed
again. The entire issue vanished when international oil prices
dropped later in the year.

A line for gasoline in northern London snakes down the street on November 3, 2000. The government's statements about blockades of fuel supplies by fuel-tax protesters led to a panic among consumers. Tony Blair considered ordering troops to supply the gas stations but was persuaded not to do so.

Of course, those high prices were what had essentially caused the problem; but the public preferred the notion that their government could do something if it just would.

Meanwhile, George W. Bush had been elected president of the United States in a hotly contested election in November 2000. President Clinton gave some parting advice to Blair on his last visit to Britain as president in December 2000. It was reported that Blair asked Clinton how he should approach Bush. Clinton replied, "Be his friend. Be his best friend. Be the guy he turns to." This advice must have pleased Blair because that would have been his first instinct anyhow.

As Bush and Blair met over the following months, they discovered that in spite of considerable political party differences, they liked and respected each other. Blair knew that Britain needed America more than the other way round but found that it wasn't such a difficult partnership with Bush after all.

January 2001 brought a new Peter Mandelson crisis. It was alleged that Mandelson had attempted to influence policy over the possible citizenship of an Indian businessman in 1999. This businessman and his brothers had later donated £1 million for sponsorship of part of the Millennium Dome. The dome had been under Mandelson's ministerial supervision at the time.

In the end, an investigation showed that there was no proof that Mandelson had done anything unethical, but it was too late. Blair was tired of fixing Mandelson problems, and consequently his old friend and advisor resigned from the cabinet. Mandelson's influence over Blair had greatly decreased by this time, but Gordon Brown was probably still smiling when the news broke. At last he was rid of the Mandelson thorn.

The tricky decision of when to call a general election was coming up in 2001. All parties in power try to use this timing to their best advantage. Since election campaign periods are short, only five or six weeks, the timing is considered crucial. Blair was on schedule for a May 1 election until a new crisis arose.

On February 20, 2001, the first case of foot-and-mouth disease was confirmed in British livestock. The outbreak escalated quickly until it was almost out of control. It could be stopped quickly only by slaughtering all affected animals and those near them. The gory sight of dead animals piled up waiting for disposal was a haunting scene.

The election was postponed because the electorate's mind couldn't be on politics when such a crisis was under way, or at least that was the accepted way to look at it. After the tide was

Foot and mouth disease took an enormous toll on British commerce and caused the postponement of the 2001 general election. This photograph shows the burning of cattle corpses at Home Farm in Poneland, Northumberland, in late February 2001. At this point, 22 farms and slaughterhouses were known to be affected.

turned with the foot-and-mouth, the election was rescheduled for June 7, 2001.

The campaign was pretty mundane except for one exciting day, May 16. On that day, Blair was scolded publicly by a constituent during a hospital visit, Deputy Leader John Prescott punched an egg-throwing protester, and Home Secretary Jack Straw was heckled at an appearance. Prescott's left jab dominated the press coverage for some days to come.

Labour expected to win, and the public agreed. Blair hadn't delivered completely on many of his 1997 promises, but he had made a start. He campaigned on the proposition that he needed more time to finish the job. The election turnout was quite small but had the expected result. Tony Blair would have another go at modernizing his party and his country.

There was no doubt that Blair needed more time to confirm the legacy that he wanted to leave behind. He had accomplished many things, including a couple that were on a historic level. His work in securing the Good Friday Agreement in Northern Ireland and his part in pushing NATO to action in Kosovo qualified him for membership in the made-history club.

Blair's problem, if it could truly be called a problem, was that there was no coherent theme to his deeds. He had taken many steps toward reforming his party and nudging his country toward social democracy, but the euro still hadn't been adopted, long waits for medical attention were common, and the transportation system needed help. He needed a focus that played to his strengths rather than to his cautious nature. He found that in a most unexpected and horrifying way.

SEPTEMBER 11, 2001

Prime Minister Blair was in a hotel room polishing a speech he was scheduled to give shortly to the Trades Union Congress in Brighton when the first plane hit the World Trade Center in New York City on September 11, 2001. Shortly after he heard of the attack, he spoke to the delegates:

> There have been most terrible, shocking events taking place in the United States of America within the last hour or so, including two hijacked planes being flown deliberately into the World Trade Centre. I'm afraid we can only imagine the terror and the carnage there, and the many, many innocent people that will have lost their lives. I know that you would want to join with me in sending the deepest condolences to President Bush and to the American people on behalf of the British people at these terrible events.

By the time of the collapse of the first tower, Prime Minister Blair was on his way back to London. Once there, he began emergency meetings with members of his cabinet and other governmental agencies. One of the biggest concerns for all world leaders during the first hours after the attack on the United States was the safety of their own cities. Blair was no exception. In the statement he gave after his return to London, he spoke of the security measures he had ordered. "We have stepped up security at airports to the highest levels. No flights will take off from the United Kingdom for which we cannot apply the highest standards of security for air crew and passengers."

All defense facilities around the world, as well as the United Kingdom police, had been put on high alert. Financial and business institutions were advised about security measures. In spite of the fear that British citizens had to feel, Blair assured them that most businesses and everyday life could go on as normal. The emotion he felt about the attack once more spilled out with his strong words. "As for those that carried out these attacks, there are no adequate words of condemnation. Their barbarism will stand as their shame for all eternity."

Blair offered up his support and his country's in words that stirred his own country and America. "This is not a battle between the United States of America and terrorism, but between the free and democratic world and terrorism. We, therefore, here in Britain stand shoulder to shoulder with our American friends in this hour of tragedy, and we, like them, will not rest until this evil is driven from our world."

It quickly became apparent that Blair was not planning to end his support with eloquent words. He recalled Parliament from a recess on September 14 and detailed the attacks to them. He listed the things that Britain and other nations must do as soon as possible, which included bringing those responsible to justice with full cooperation between all countries. He finished his speech with a firm statement of belief. "Our beliefs are the very opposite of the fanatics. We believe in reason, democracy, and tolerance. These beliefs are the foundation of our civilised world. They are enduring, they have served us well and as history has shown we have been prepared to fight when necessary to defend them."

In the following days and weeks, Blair didn't back off from "standing shoulder to shoulder" with America.

Blair began calling foreign leaders immediately to help build a coalition of nations to combat terrorism. Shortly after that, he began weeks of traveling to firm up the coalition. His first stop was America, where he talked with President Bush and visited Congress. Blair sat beside First Lady Laura Bush in the gallery as President Bush addressed a joint session of Congress. Bush paid tribute in his speech to Blair and Great Britain and their friendship with the United States.

Blair set out his aims for the fight against terrorism early and stuck to them. He repeatedly made it clear that the blame for the attack should not be laid at the feet of all Muslims but rather an extremist few. In a statement given on September 25, Blair said, "Our fight is not with Islam. Our fight is with a terrorist network and a regime that sustains them in mutual support. The vast majority of Muslims, as I've said many times before, condemn the attacks as unreservedly as we do."

As it became increasingly evident that Osama bin Laden and the al Qaeda terrorist network were responsible for the attack, Blair voiced over and over that the Taliban regime in Afghanistan must yield up bin Laden and his associates. He committed Britain to help in any way that the United States wanted, including military help.

He also promised the assembly of a humanitarian coalition to support refugees in and outside of Afghanistan. "There are two million refugees in Pakistan and one and a half million in Iran. We have to act for humanitarian reasons to alleviate the appalling suffering of the Afghan people and deliver stability so that people from that region stay in that region."

President Bush meets with Prime Minister Tony Blair in the Blue Room at the White House in Washington, D.C., on September 20, 2001. The meeting took place days after the September 11th attacks on the United States, and hours before Bush would address Congress and the nation.

At a subdued Labour Party conference in Brighton on October 2, Blair spoke of the opportunity to make good come of evil. "This is a moment to seize. The kaleidoscope has been shaken. The pieces are in flux. Soon they will settle again. Before they do, let us re-order this world around us."

Blair set out to fulfill his promise to the United States. He crisscrossed Europe, the Middle East, and parts of Asia, talking to leaders, urging them to join the coalition to fight terror. Most countries pledged their support in one way or another. By the time the first air and missile strikes began against terrorist targets in Afghanistan on October 7, Blair had helped firm the resolve of countries such as Pakistan, Russia, and China, who might have been lukewarm toward military action in Afghanistan.

Operation Veritas was the British code name for the military operation undertaken in and near Afghanistan. Initially, Royal Navy submarines launched Tomahawk missiles to hit terrorist training camps in Afghanistan. After the first missiles, the Royal Air Force (RAF) provided support with air-to-air refueling of U.S. aircraft. The RAF also flew reconnaissance and surveillance missions during the weeks of bombing.

Support for Blair's actions among his own countrymen was strong on the whole. The Conservative leader, Iain Duncan Smith, had virtually no criticism for Blair's actions or plans. Not surprisingly, some of the strongest opposition came from within Blair's own party. After the first flush of anger at the attacks, there was disagreement about exposing Britain to similar attack simply by aligning so strongly with the United States. Blair appeared unaware of that line of thought.

The usually cautious Blair, who judged the effect of every political decision carefully, threw that caution to the winds. His sense of the moral rightness of his position and consequent actions on behalf of Britain was unshakable. The public's opinion of him was high, and he had just won reelection—so any criticism was largely blunted.

In December, the International Security Assistance Force, with UN sanction, was formed to assist the new government in Afghanistan. British major general John McColl was appointed the commander of the multinational force. Britain agreed to send a peacekeeping force of between 1,000 and 1,500 troops.

It was finally time to get back to the sticky problems at home, which seemed more difficult at times than ridding the world of terrorism. Prime Minister Blair's New Year's message reflected pride at what had been accomplished since September 11 and determination to carry on with the fight.

He spoke of his hope that Britain's economic growth could be maintained in spite of the downturn in many other countries, including the United States. Improving schools and the transport system were two of his priorities. He concluded that Britain had "big challenges." He continued, "But on our strong economic foundations, with proper investment now going into our public services, with the right arguments about the type of society we want, with Britain growing stronger in the world, with the right values for today, I am confident that we are well placed to meet them."

10

The War on Terror

PRIME MINISTER BLAIR MAY HAVE WANTED TO TURN TO DOMESTIC ISSUES in early 2002, after the frenzy of travel and negotiating of the previous fall, but world events worked against that. The focus remained on the Middle East. It appeared that the war in Afghanistan had gone well. The Taliban had been banished from Afghanistan, and the Afghan people had begun taking tiny steps toward democracy.

The war on terror had destroyed the vipers' nests of al Qaeda training camps in Afghanistan and sent the terrorists scrambling for cover in other nearby countries. Osama bin Laden was still on the loose, but his ability to direct further attacks seemed to have been removed.

To many European leaders and their people, Afghanistan was a job well done. It had been the right thing to do and seemed to have been executed very well. It was time to move on. This wasn't the view held by the United States. Soon the buzz in world capitals was all about the United States invading Iraq.

Most nations had deplored the devastation of 9/11 in the United States, but few supported further military action. Their reasoning was that there was no absolute proof that Iraq and Saddam Hussein had played any direct role in the 9/11 attacks. They also thought that the containment policies currently being used with Hussein and Iraq were working.

President George Bush disagreed strongly and wanted to see some major changes in Iraq, which included Saddam Hussein being ousted as president. Bush and many other U.S. leaders were certain that Iraq possessed weapons of mass destruction. Saddam had previously used chemical weapons on some of his own people, and it was commonly believed that he also had biological weapons and was developing nuclear ones.

In contrast to other European leaders, Tony Blair saw no way that life or government could go back to pre-9/11 days. He believed that nations must join together in multilateral alliances to defeat the terrorists who wanted to destroy Western civilization. Blair certainly didn't want war with Iraq, but he did not go back on his promise to support the United States in its fight against terrorism.

Blair's attitude made the alarm bells ring even louder in London when talk of war rose to a fever pitch after President Bush gave his State of the Union address to the U.S. Congress late in January. Bush caused a tremendous stir by naming Iraq, Iran, and North Korea as parts of an "axis of evil." Many British leaders and their European counterparts considered this to be reckless rhetoric even if it was true.

Blair made two visits to the United States in 2002. He visited President Bush's Crawford, Texas, ranch in April to talk over the Iraq situation. The media called the meeting a war council. It was true that the U.S. position on Iraq seemed to have hardened into a definite preference for regime change in

Korean farmers burn U.S. flags during a protest against the United States in downtown Seoul on February 20, 2002. The protestors were reacting to President Bush's reference to North Korea being part of an "axis of evil."

that country. Bush made that clear in his press conferences, but the how and when of the change was not definite. Blair hoped to influence the method and timing of any military action.

During his visit, Blair gave a speech at nearby College Station. In it, he set out his views quite clearly. "We must be prepared to act where terrorism or weapons of mass destruction threaten us . . . if necessary the action should be military and again, if necessary and justified, it should involve regime change." He went on to say of Saddam: "To allow WMD [weapons of mass destruction] to be developed by a state like Iraq without let or hindrance would be grossly to ignore the lessons of September 11 and we will not do it."

The tension over war built through the summer until it seemed a certainty. When Blair visited Bush at Camp David in early September, he didn't try to talk the president out of military action. Instead, he asked Bush to take action through the UN. Blair wanted the UN Security Council to pass a resolution calling for Saddam Hussein to allow weapons inspectors back into Iraq. Blair knew that Bush was under pressure from some of his advisors to skip the UN resolution route and wanted Bush's assurance that he would go to the international body.

Blair's position was that war in Iraq needed the approval of the international community. Part of the UN's reason for existence was to police member nations. Saddam's record for persecuting his own people, using chemical weapons, and starting wars certainly seemed reason enough for the UN to get involved. As both Blair and Bush knew, it wasn't that simple. Economic and political reasons might keep the Security Council from doing anything definite with Saddam. Many nations wanted to leave well enough alone.

Blair also knew that his own country's leaders and the citizens would more easily support a war if the UN approved. Public opinion against military action in Iraq had steadily hardened over the summer.

TONY BLAIR LATER SAID THAT THE REPORT WAS "AN ABSOLUTELY CLEAR SIGN THAT [SADDAM] HAD NO INTENTION OF SHUTTING THIS STUFF DOWN."

Prime Minister Blair was relieved when Bush went before the UN on September 12, 2002, and asked that the Security Council pass a new resolution, calling for Saddam to allow weapons inspectors back into Iraq. After much wrangling and bargaining among Security Council members, UN Resolution 1441 was passed on November 8, 2002. The resolution stated that Saddam had one final opportunity to comply with the UN by letting inspectors back into Iraq to make sure that there weren't any weapons of mass destruction.

Tension eased at home in Britain for Tony Blair, at least for a while. The UN was in control and that was the only way that Blair thought he could gain support for going to war alongside the United States if it came to that.

Resolution 1441 wasn't perfect because it didn't spell out what would happen next if Saddam didn't comply or even how to measure his compliance. By January, the United States was insisting that Saddam hadn't complied as required. The United States continued to ship troops and materials to the Middle East in a massive buildup prior to a military action.

Saddam had issued a 12,000-page report in December that supposedly detailed his dismantling of his weapons program, and inspectors had been allowed back into Iraq. They hadn't found any WMD, yet but the search had just begun. The report was mostly old information, but now the UN had yet another dilemma. Had he complied or hadn't he?

Bush and Blair held similar opinions about the answer to that question. Blair later said that the report was "an absolutely clear sign that [Saddam] had no intention of shutting this stuff down." He believed that this was the time to present Iraq with a "clear ultimatum."

One of Blair's clearest goals during this time was to maintain the international alliance that Resolution 1441 had supposedly created. However, by January, France and Germany had begun to backtrack, and the relative vagueness of the resolution didn't help.

Blair traveled again to Washington, D.C., at the end of January 2002 to make a couple of requests of President Bush. Blair wanted Bush to support a second resolution in the UN that authorized military consequences for Iraq's noncompliance, and he wanted more time—time to convince Saddam to leave and time to rally Britain's citizens to the cause of war. Bush was unable to give Blair definite promises to go along with the two requests.

The prime minister went home to begin six weeks of diplomacy within his own political party and as a go-between to try to convince the nonpermanent UN Security Council members to agree to a second resolution. The five permanent Security Council members are the United States, Britain, China, France, and Russia. Other members of the UN General Assembly rotate for terms on the Security Council. China, France, and Russia seemed unlikely to vote for another resolution, so the vote would rest on some of the nonpermanent members, who at that time were Syria, Germany, Mexico, Chile, Pakistan, Cameroon, Angola, and Guinea.

Blair used every bit of his personal persuasiveness and even charm to attempt to build a majority within the Security Council. He also did everything he could to persuade his own Labour Party members to support a possible war with Iraq. For the first time in his political career, Blair found it rough going to bring others around to his point of view. It was an exhausting and discouraging time for him.

By the end of the first week in March, it looked like Britain and the United States wouldn't be able to get the votes

Ambassadors arrive to vote on a new Iraq resolution on November 8, 2002 at the United Nations. The security council unanimously approved the resolution, forcing Saddam Hussein to disarm or face serious consequences that would undoubtedly lead to war.

to pass a second resolution. As Blair had promised his party that there would be a second UN resolution, this was not the news he wanted to hear from Jack Straw, who was now foreign secretary. Straw had returned from New York with this news after yet another meeting of the Security Council.

In the midst of the crisis, which threatened Blair's survival, there were a couple of helpful events. Military action had been delayed as Blair desired, although it may have been because of unexpected slowness in achieving the desired buildup of troops and supplies by the U.S. military rather than because of Blair's request.

It also helped that French president Jacques Chirac announced on March 10 that France would veto any attempt to pass a second UN resolution. Chirac said that France would block authorization for military action "in all circumstances." Blair interpreted this as being an unreasonable veto and proposed that the existing resolutions therefore provided authorization for war. It was a tricky move, but it worked.

Blair gave two speeches on March 18, first to his own Labour Party members of Parliament and then to the entire House of Commons. He spoke eloquently and passionately in favor of going to war with the United States against Iraq. He told his fellow Labour MPs, "Don't vote for me out of loyalty. Vote for me because it's the right thing to do."

He told the House of Commons, "This is the time . . . to show that we will confront the tyrannies and dictatorships and terrorists who put our way of life at risk, to show at the moment of decision that we have the courage to do the right thing."

At the end of the debate, the vote was taken. Labour MPs hadn't all been convinced—139 had voted against Blair, but the vote was still won. A day later, Britain went to war alongside the United States.

11

Aftermath of War

OVER 46,000 BRITISH TROOPS WENT TO WAR DURING THE INVASION OF Iraq. The war went better than Blair could have expected, at least from a military viewpoint. British soldiers were given an important role, and while there were many casualties, the number was much less than anticipated. Within three weeks, Iraqis in Baghdad had torn down a huge statue of Saddam Hussein that stood in a city square. In another three weeks, President George Bush proclaimed the end of major hostilities.

The spring and early summer of 2003 were good times for Blair. Public opinion in Britain had rallied behind Blair and the British troops in the war zone. There were still many who remained against the war, but even Blair's opponents admired that he hadn't backed down from doing what he believed to be right.

The good times started to sour in June when evidence that Saddam had weapons of mass destruction still hadn't appeared.

Tony Blair bolsters the spirits of troops in Iraq on May 29, 2003.

The threat of WMD was the foremost reason that Blair had used to convince the MPs and the British people that Britain needed to go to war against Iraq. Blair himself thought that regime change was enough reason, but he knew that his position wasn't shared by most politicians and citizens in Britain.

The British Broadcasting Corporation, usually called just the BBC, aired a television report in June saying that Blair's office had embellished an intelligence report in September 2002. The BBC claimed that Blair's office made the WMD threat seem worse than it was in order to convince MPs and the public that going to war was the only answer.

Pressure had already begun building against the war as the occupation of Iraq by coalition forces wasn't going smoothly.

Saddam hadn't been caught, and soldiers were being killed by insurgent soldiers almost every day. Blair's opponents remembered now that they had been against this war from the start.

The real tragedy of the BBC accusation happened in July within 24 hours of what may have been one of the highlights of Blair's career. He spoke on July 17, 2003, to a joint session of the U.S. Congress. President Bush had just presented Blair with the Medal of Freedom, the highest civilian honor that the president can bestow. The Congress and the American people had given Blair a rousing welcome in appreciation for his willingness to stand with America in the fight in Iraq.

On July 18, the body of Dr. David Kelly, a British government weapons expert, was found in a field in Oxfordshire, where he had apparently committed suicide. Dr. Kelly had been accused of being a source for the BBC report. Although Dr. Kelly hadn't been accused of wrongdoing, he had been under immense and unaccustomed pressure.

Prime Minister Blair immediately appointed Lord Hutton to head up an independent inquiry into Dr. Kelly's death. Lord Hutton called many witnesses, including Blair, and published his report on January 28, 2004. Hutton found no evidence of wrongdoing on the part of the government. He also found no evidence that the BBC's claims of embellishment to the intelligence report were true.

Lord Hutton, however, declined to offer any opinions about the state of prewar intelligence gathering. He said it was not part of his responsibility. Hutton's report was rather unexpectedly supportive of the government's version of the events, which led opponents to call the report a whitewash. The BBC chairman plus two other employees resigned in the aftermath of the report.

On August 1, in the midst of the uproar over Dr. Kelly's suicide, Blair passed a milestone. He became the longest continuously serving Labour prime minister. Former prime minister Harold Wilson had served a longer total, but his terms had been broken up into chunks of service. There was no celebration because of Dr. Kelly's death, but it was a momentous occasion just the same.

In October 2003, it seemed that Blair was paying a price for the stress of the last two years when he was briefly hospitalized with tachycardia, or irregular heartbeat. His condition was treated successfully with cardioversion, but a year later, he had to undergo a catheter ablation to further treat the same condition.

During this same time period, Blair's longtime communications director and political advisor, Alastair Campbell, left. Campbell said that his departure had been planned for some time, but it was still a loss to the ailing prime minister. Blair's longevity in office was taking a toll on his ministers as they tired of the pace of public life in Prime Minister Blair's government. It wasn't a good fall for Blair, leading to much speculation that he might resign.

Things looked up in January with the release of the Hutton Report and with the Butler Report release in July 2004. The Butler Report was initiated by Blair shortly after the Hutton Report was released. Lord Butler headed a five-member committee that looked into the intelligence relating to Iraq's weapons of mass destruction. This intelligence had been a key factor in Britain's decision to go to war against Iraq. Ten months had passed since Saddam fell from power and still no WMD had been found.

The Butler Review Committee met in secret and reviewed all aspects of intelligence gathering and how it led to the conclusions about Iraq. The final report stated that the key intelligence used to prove that Iraq had WMD was not substantial enough to use as justification for war. However, they found no particular individuals to be at fault, including Prime Minister Blair.

The WMD issue continued to cause trouble for Blair, and in August 2004, MP Adam Price announced that he would seek

MP Adam Price is pictured with his report, "A Case to Answer," in Westminster, England, on August 26, 2004. Price attempted to impeach Tony Blair for misleading the country over the case for war with Iraq.

Blair's impeachment for misleading the British people and using faulty intelligence to go to war. Impeachment for abuse of power is part of British parliamentary law but hadn't been used for 150 years. In the end, Price was not able to secure enough support among the MPs to start impeachment proceedings, but it was a nasty episode for Blair just the same.

Meanwhile, domestic issues continued to call for Blair's attention. He announced in April 2004 that he had changed his mind about calling a referendum election for voting on the ratification of the European Constitution. A referendum vote in favor of the constitution was seen as a long shot, and Blair wanted to maintain close ties to the EU. In what was probably an effort to avoid a negative vote, he had previously stated that he didn't see a reason for a vote on the new EU Constitution since it wouldn't fundamentally alter Britain's relationship with the EU.

The reasons for Blair's change of heart were not fully explained, but this turnabout gave more ammunition to his opponents. The referendum was expected to be held in early 2006, but in 2005, the constitution was rejected by French and Dutch voters. With ratification then in doubt anyhow, the referendum plans were put on hold.

In September and early October 2004, Blair laid out his plans for two major issues: climate change and poverty in Africa. In 2005, he was scheduled to be both the president of the EU and the G8 organizations. He announced that his main agendas during both presidencies would deal with solutions for climate change and how to help rid Africa of the grinding poverty it has among its people.

The fall of 2004 was also campaign time in the United States. John Kerry seemed to have a good chance to defeat George Bush in the November election. Bush's incumbent standing was threatened by opposition to the continuing bloodshed in Iraq. Saddam had been captured, and the Iraqis had taken over their own government, but the promised weapons of mass destruction still hadn't turned up.

How would a John Kerry victory affect Prime Minister Blair? Blair had risked his political survival when he threw his and Britain's support behind President Bush and the Iraq war. Blair's opponents thought a Kerry presidency might force Blair out sooner than the next election. The Labour Party usually aligned itself with Democrats in the United States, and that had always been part of the puzzlement that Blair's fellow Labour Party members felt over Blair's staunch friendship with Bush. George Bush won reelection, and it seemed that Blair's fortunes began to turn around about that time.

On February 6, 2005, Blair reached another longevity milestone. He became the longest-serving Labour prime minister. His 2,838 days in office took him past even the total service of Harold Wilson.

It was time for Blair to call an election, and the polling date was set for May 5, 2005. It was a hard-fought campaign as many British citizens still opposed the war in Iraq and blamed Blair for getting Britain involved. Blair did win, but the margin was much less than in any of his two previous elections. Labour lost 47 seats in Parliament and received only 35 percent of the popular vote, but the party retained its majority. This diminished mandate led some of Blair's own party members to call for his departure sooner rather than later. Gordon Brown remained the front-runner to take Blair's place, and some Labour MPs thought it was time to make the change.

But as often happens, events did the changing. The July 7 bombing reminded politicians and citizens alike that Prime Minister Blair was the right man to be in charge when terrorists targeted your homeland. His ability to manage the crisis, chair the G8 summit, and comfort the bereaved and injured all within a few days reassured Britons and cemented Blair's probability of serving out a full third term.

Within days of the bombings, several suspects had been identified. More bomb blasts on July 21 frightened Londoners, but the devices were cruder and the damage was much less.

After being reelected for a third term, Tony Blair poses outside his home with his wife, Cherie, and his youngest son, Leo, on May 6, 2005.

Blair said the bombings were intended "to scare people and to frighten them, to make them anxious and worried." He added, "Police have done their very best, and the security services too, in the situation, and I think we have just got to react calmly and continue with our business as much as possible as normal."

The July 21 bombs were not suicide bombs, and the terrorists believed to have been responsible were soon tracked down and charged. The attacks and their aftermath had demonstrated much strength in London, including the rapid response by rescuers and the dozens of surveillance cameras in tube stations that had helped the police identify the terrorists.

The British have been targeted with bombs in the past during World War II and more recently from the Irish Republican Army. Perhaps that's part of the reason they showed such calm in the midst of tragedy. Prime Minister Blair expressed great admiration for his fellow Londoners, who carried on their lives with grim determination.

Blair's place as a world leader has been confirmed over and over in the eight years he has been in office. His insistence that his country "do the right thing" when confronted with terrorist attacks showed his daring. Perhaps his determination to go against his own political party showed his true courage. He has made mistakes, as he admits, but history will be the judge of those and of Tony Blair's place in the hall of great British prime ministers.

CHRONOLOGY

1953	Anthony Charles Lynton Blair is born in Edinburgh, Scotland, on May 6.
1961–1966	Attends Chorister School in Durham.
1966–1971	Attends Fettes College in Edinburgh.
1972–1975	Attends St. John's College, Oxford.
1975	One-year course at Lincoln's Inn Law School.
1980	Marries Cherie Booth on March 29.
1983	Elected MP for Sedgefield on June 9.
1984	Appointed to shadow treasury team on November 7.
1987	Appointed as deputy to shadow trade and industry secretary on July 8.
1988	Elected to shadow cabinet, appointed as energy secretary on November 10.
1989	Appointed as shadow employment secretary in November.
1992	Appointed as shadow home secretary.
1994	Elected as leader of Labour Party on July 21.
1997	Labour Party wins general election on May 1.
1997	Appointed as prime minister on May 2.
2001	Labour Party wins general election June 7; Blair gets second term.
2005	Labour Party wins general election May 5; Blair gets third term.
2005	Takes over as rotating president of the European Union on July 1.
2005	Chairs G8 summit in Gleneagles, Scotland, on July 8.
2006	Local elections result in the loss of 317 seats and 18 councils in Blair's administration.

PHOTO CREDITS

INDEX

About the Authors

BONNIE HINMAN graduated from Missouri State University in Springfield in 1972. She has taught creative writing at Crowder College in Neosho, Missouri, and is the author of 15 books. This book is her fifth biography for Chelsea House Publishers. The author lives in Joplin, Missouri, with her husband, Bill, and near her grown son and daughter and grandson, Will.

ARTHUR M. SCHLESINGER, JR. is the leading American historian of our time. He won the Pulitzer Prize for his books *The Age of Jackson* (1945) and *A Thousand Days* (1965), which also won the National Book Award. Professor Schlesinger is the Albert Schweitzer Professor of the Humanities at the City University of New York and has been involved in several other Chelsea House projects, including the series *Revolutionary War Leaders*, *Colonial Leaders*, and *Your Government*.